STUDIA GRAECA ET LATINA LUNDENSIA 6

St. Bridget's Revelations to the Popes

An edition of the so-called *Tractatus de summis pontificibus*

Arne Jönsson

GW00535808

Lund
University
Press

Published with the aid of grants from the Hjalmar Gullberg
and Greta Thott research fund

Lund University Press
Box 141
SE-221 00 Lund
Sweden

Art nr 20452
ISSN 1100-7931
ISBN 91-7966-399-0 Lund University Press
ISBN 0-86238-470-2 Chartwell-Bratt Ltd

Printed in Sweden
Studentlitteratur
Lund 1997

VXORI
OPTIMAE

Table of contents

Bibliography

Manuscripts

F = *Lund*, Universitetsbiblioteket, ms. 21 ("Codex Falkenberg"), late 14th century.
(**Gh** = *editio princeps*, printed by B. Ghotan, Lübeck 1492.)
K = *Kalmar*, Stifts- och Gymnasiebiblioteket, late 14th century.
L = *London*, British Library, ms. Harley 612, middle 15th century.
p = *Stockholm*, Royal Library, ms. A22, first half of the 15th century.
q = *Vienna*, Nationalbibliothek, ms. 3960, dated 1380-1386.
y = *Prague*, Universitní Knihovna, ms. V. G. 20, late 14th century.
W^b = *Florence*, Biblioteca Medicea Laurenziana, ms. Ashb. 896, early 15th century.
Z^a = *Helsinki*, University Library, "Codex Nordenskiöld", early 15th century.

Printed works

Acta et Processus Canonizacionis Beate Birgitte. Utg. av I. Collijn (*SSFS*, Ser. 2, Latinska skrifter I), Uppsala 1924-31.
Alfonso of Jaén, *Epistola solitarii* and *Informaciones*. See Jönsson, *Alfonso of Jaén*.
— *Conscripcio de eleccione Urbani sexti.* See Bliemetzrieder, pp. 83-100.
Aili, H., *Rev. IV.* See Birgitta.
— 'St. Birgitta and the Text of the *Revelationes*. A Survey of Some Influences Traceable to Translators and Editors'. See *The Editing of Theological and Philosophical Texts*, pp. 75-91.
Bergh, B., *Palaeography and Textual Criticism* (*Scripta Minora Regiae Societatis Humaniorum Litterarum Lundensis, Studier utgivna av Kungl. Humanistiska Vetenskapssamfundet i Lund* 1979-1980:2), Lund 1978.
— *Rev. V-VII.* See Birgitta.
— 'Zeitdifferenzbestimmungen mit *per* in birgittinischen Texten', *Eranos* 64 (1966), p. 133-148.
Birgitta, Sancta, *Quattuor Oraciones* (*Opera Minora III*). Edited by S. Eklund (*KVHAA* and *SSFS*, Ser. 2, Latinska skrifter VIII:3), Arlöv 1991.
— *Regula Salvatoris* (*Opera Minora I*). Edited by S. Eklund (*KVHAA* and *SSFS*, Ser. 2, Latinska skrifter VIII:1), Uppsala 1975.

— *Reuelaciones, Book I with Magister Mathias' Prologue,* edited by C.-G. Undhagen (*KVHAA* and *SSFS*, Ser. 2, Latinska skrifter VII:1), Stockholm 1977.

— *Reuelaciones, Book III,* edited by A.-M. Jönsson (forthcoming)

— *Reuelaciones, Book IV,* edited by H. Aili (*KVHAA* and *SSFS*, Ser. 2, Latinska skrifter VII:4), Göteborg 1992.

— *Reuelaciones, Book V, Liber questionum,* edited by Birger Bergh (*KVHAA* and *SSFS*, Ser. 2, Latinska skrifter VII:5), Uppsala 1971.

— *Reuelaciones, Book VI,* edited by B. Bergh (*KVHAA* and *SSFS*, Ser. 2, Latinska skrifter VII:6), Arlöv 1991.

— *Reuelaciones, Bok VII,* edited by B. Bergh (*KVHAA* and *SSFS*, Ser. 2, Latinska skrifter VII:7), diss., Uppsala 1967.

— *Reuelaciones extrauagantes.* Edited by L. Hollman (*SSFS*, Ser. 2, Latinska skrifter V), diss., Uppsala 1956.

— *Revelationes S. Birgittae e codice membr. fol. 21 Bibl. Universitatis Lundensis* edidit E. Wessén, 1-2 (*Corpus codicum Suecicorum medii aevi* XIII-XIV), Hafniae 1952-56).

— *Revelationes.* Impressit B. Ghotan. Lubece 1492.

— *Sermo Angelicus (Opera Minora II).* Edited by S. Eklund (*KVHAA* and *SSFS*, Ser. 2, Latinska skrifter VIII:2), Uppsala 1972.

Birgitta of Sweden, Life and Selected Revelations. Edited, with a preface by Marguerite Tjader Harris, translation and notes by Albert Ryle Kezel, introduction by Tore Nyberg (*The Classics of Western Spirituality*), New York, Mahwah 1990.

Bliemetzrieder, F. P., 'Un'altra edizione rifatta del trattato di Alfonso Pecha, vescovo resignato di Iaën, sullo scisma (1387-88), con notizie sulla vita di Pietro Bohier, Benedettino, vescovo di Orvieto', *Rivista storica benedettina* 4 (1909), pp. 74-100.

Colledge, E., '*Epistola solitarii ad reges.* Alphonse of Pecha as Organizer of Birgittine and Urbanist Propaganda', *Mediaeval Studies* 18 (1956), pp. 19-49.

The Editing of Theological and Philosophical Texts from the Middle Ages. Acts of the Conference Arranged by the Department of Classical Languages, University of Stockholm, 29-31 August 1984. Edited by Monika Asztalos (*AUS, SLS* 30), Stockholm 1986.

Eklund, S., *Regula Salvatoris,* see Birgitta.

Ekwall, S., *Vår äldsta Birgittavita och dennas viktigaste varianter* (*KVHAAH, Historiska serien* 12), Lund 1965.

— 'Quando morì il B. Giovanni dalle Celle?', *Rivista di Storia della Chiesa in Italia* 1951, pp. 371-374.

Ellis, R., 'The Divine Message and its Human Agents; St. Birgitta and her editors'. See *Studies in St. Birgitta,* pp. 209-233.

Gilkær, H. T., *The Political Ideas of St. Birgitta and her Spanish Confessor, Alfonso Pecha. Liber Celestis Imperatoris ad Reges: A Mirror of Princes* (*Odense University Studies in History and Social Sciences* 163), Odense 1993.

— 'Redaktionelle problemer i Åbenbaringernes VIII bog. Bogens disposition: Alfons Pechas ordningsprincipper', *Birgitta, hendes værk og hendes klostre i Norden*, edited by Tore Nyberg (*Odense University Studies in History and Social Sciences* 150), Odense 1991, pp. 425-46.

Grundmann, H., 'Die Papstprophetien des Mittelalters', in idem: *Ausgewählte Aufsätze*, II (*Schriften der Monumenta Germaniae Historica* 25,2), Stuttgart 1977, pp. 1-57.

Hollman, L., *Den Heliga Birgittas Reuelaciones extrauagantes*. See Birgitta.

Jönsson, A., *Alfonso of Jaén. His Life and Works with Critical Editions of the Epistola Solitarii, the Informaciones and the Epistola Serui Christi* (*Studia Graeca et Latina Lundensia* 1), diss., Lund 1989.

— 'Birgitta i Birgittalegenderna', *Heliga Birgitta — budskapet och förebilden*. Edited by Alf Härdelin and Mereth Lindgren (*KVHAA*, Konferenser 28), pp. 35-48.

— [Review of] *H. T. Gilkær, The Political Ideas...*, *Historisk Tidskrift* 1995, pp. 116-120.

— 'On the so-called *Tractatus de summis pontificibus*', *Birgittiana* 1 (1996), pp. 15-27.

Jörgensen, A., 'En Birgitta-handskrift i Helsingfors universitetsbibliotek', *Miscellanea bibliographica* I (*Helsingfors universitetsbiblioteks skrifter* VIII), Helsingfors 1925, pp. 19-67.

Klockars, B., *Birgitta och böckerna. En undersökning av den heliga Birgittas källor* (*KVHAAH*, Historiska serien 11), Lund 1966.

— *Birgitta och hennes värld* (*KVHAAH*, Historiska serien 16), Stockholm 1971.

— *Biskop Hemming av Åbo* (*Skrifter utgivna av Svenska litteratursällskapet i Finland* 379), diss., Vasa 1960.

Mathias, Magister, Prologus. See Birgitta, *Reuelaciones, Book I*.

Nyberg, T., *Birgitta of Sweden*, see *Birgitta of Sweden*.

— *Birgittinische Klostergründungen des Mittelalters* (*Bibliotheca Historica Lundensis* XV), diss., Lund 1965.

— *Birgittinsk festgåva. Studier on heliga Birgitta och Birgittinorden* (*Skrifter utgivna av Svenska Kyrkohistoriska Föreningen* 46), Uppsala 1991.

Öberg, J., 'Authentischer oder autorisierter Text? Der Weg von Konzept zu moderner Edition an Beispielen von Petrus de Dacia und der Heiligen Birgitta'. See *The Editing of Theological and Philosophical Texts*, pp. 59-74.

— *Kring Birgitta* (*KVHAA*, Filologiskt arkiv 13), Lund 1969.

Oxford Latin Dictionary, Oxford 1968-82.

Piltz, A., 'Communicantes. Aspekter på kyrkan som solidarisk gemenskap i svensk högmedeltid', *Svensk spiritualitet. Tio studier av förhållandet tro-kyrka-praxis*, Klippan 1994, pp. 15-55.

Schmid, T., *Birgitta och hennes uppenbarelser*, Lund 1940.

Schück, H., *Några anmärkningar om Birgittas revelationer* (*KVHAAH* 33, Ny följd 13:1), Stockholm 1901.

Sensi, M., 'Alfonso Pecha e l'eremitismo italiano di fine secolo XIV', *Rivista di Storia della Chiesa in Italia* 47 (1993), pp. 51-80.

Studies in St. Birgitta and the Brigittine Order, edited by James Hogg, vol. 1 (*Analecta Cartusiana* 35: 19, *Spiritualität heute und gestern* 19), Salzburg 1993.

Thesaurus Linguae Latinae, I-, Lipsiae 1900-.

Undhagen, C.-G., *Rev. I*, see Birgitta.

— 'Une source du prologue (Chap. 1) aux Révélations de Sainte Brigitte par le cardinal Jean de Turrecremata', *Eranos* 58 (1960), pp. 214-226.

Voaden, R., 'The Middle English *Epistola solitarii ad reges* of Alfonso of Jaen: An Edition of the Text in British Library MS Cotton Julius F ii'. See *Studies in St. Birgitta*, pp. 142-179.

Westman, K. B., *Birgitta-studier* (*Uppsala Universitets Årsskrift* 1911, Teologi 1), diss., Uppsala 1911.

Abbreviations

add.	addidit
A & P	*Acta et Processus*, see the bibliography
alt.	alteravit
AUS	*Acta Universitatis Stockholmiensis*
cf.	confer
ch.	chapter
corr.	correxit
del.	delevit
f(f).	folium (folia)
KVHAA(H)	*Kungl. Vitterhets Historie och Antikvitets Akademien(s Handlingar)*
marg.	margine
OLD	*Oxford Latin Dictionary* (see the bibliography)
om.	omisit
r.	recto
R	rubric
rec.	recensuit
rev.	revelacio, revelation
Rev. ex.	Reuelacio extrauagans
SFSS	*Samlingar utgivna av Svenska Fornskriftsällskapet*
suppl.	supplevit
SLS	*Studia Latina Stockholmiensia*
TLL	*Thesaurus Linguae Latinae* (see the bibliography)
tpt.	transposuit
v.	verso
vol.	volume
< >	supplenda
{ }	delenda

The books of the Bible are abbreviated according to the principles applied in the *Biblia Sacra iuxta Vulgatam Versionem* (rec. Weber), I-II, Stuttgart 1975.

1. Introduction

1.1. St. Bridget and the popes

In the 14th century many people, including some popes, felt that the Church was in urgent need of reform. If the Church did not embody the ideals and values of the gospel, the blame was placed on the popes, since they had been entrusted with the task of watching over the Christians. As many felt that very little was accomplished in the field of reform, the popes as persons (not the institution, of course) quickly became the object of criticism. The very fact that the popes, the bishops of Rome, resided at Avignon was an affront, and many Christians felt that the pope's return to Rome was a prerequisite for reform. Since the popes were themselves the arbiters of reform and reformers had to have papal approval to gain official status, the only alternative left to those who wanted to carry out reforms was to try to influence the popes and goad them into taking action. One of these concerned Christians was St. Bridget of Sweden. She had revelations in which God, Christ or St. Mary appeared, deploring the state of the Church in general and condemning a number of abuses and bad practices. In several revelations, the popes too are treated harshly. A famous example is book I, ch. 41. This revelation is a message from the Creator to the *caput Ecclesie mee*, viz. Pope Clement VI (1342-1352). God reminds him of the fact that he sits on His throne as successor to St. Peter and has been entrusted with the task of binding and loosening the souls from sin, but he is performing miserably. Instead of saving souls, he disperses and kills them; he is even worse than Lucifer:

> tu, qui deberes soluere animas et ad me presentare, tu vere es animarum interfector ... Tu ... es dispersor et lacerator earum, tu ... peior es Lucifero. Ipse enim habebat ad me inuidiam et nullum concupiuit occidere nisi me, ut pro me dominaretur. Tu autem tanto deterior est, quod non solum occidis me remouendo te a me per mala opera tua, sed et animas occidis per malum exemplum tuum.

There is another revelation too, VI: 63, in which Christ condemns Pope Clement for his sins and offences and exhorts him to make amends and take action. A new rubric was written to this revelation when republished (see below rev. I) and from this we learn that Bridget received the message two years before the Jubilee year, that is in 1348, and that it was communicated to the pope in Avignon by two friends of Bridget's, Bishop Hemming of Åbo and Prior Peter of Alvastra.

Bridget herself went to Rome for the Jubilee year, never to return to Sweden. In her revelations, she paints a very gloomy picture of conditions in contemporary Rome. In IV: 33, a letter to an unknown addressee, there is a long list of complaints: e. g., that churches are abandoned and converted into latrines for people, dogs and wild animals, that people eat meat in Lent, that the property of the Church is given to laymen, who do not marry because they hold the position of canons, but impudently have concubines in their houses in the day and in their beds at night, saying audaciously: 'We cannot marry, because we are canons'.

To judge from Rev III: 27, for example, Bridget seems to put the blame for this corruption on Pope Boniface VIII, whose pontificate had proved so disastrous for the Church; according to her, there had been many confessors and martyrs in the period from St. Peter to Boniface's predecessor Celestine V, but after that, development took a turn for the worse. St. Bridget thinks that the root of the problem lies in the popes' absence from Rome (in the above-mentioned revelation IV: 33 she finishes by saying that the priests are like orphans because of the pope's absence). In this perspective it is natural that she is a determined advocate of the popes' return to Rome, as is witnessed by a number of revelations (see below).

1.2. The *Tractatus de summis pontificibus*

Immediately after St. Bridget's death, her revelations were collected and edited as the *Liber celestis* and the *Liber celestis imperatoris ad reges*. The editorial work had been entrusted to her Spanish confessor, Alfonso Pecha, former Bishop of Jaén in the south of Spain.[1] In the *Liber celestis*, which was probably finished in about 1375,[2] there are some revelations in which the popes are referred to in various ways and in various contexts.[3] Some other revelations to popes and concerning popes were not published until some years later, however, in a collection that is normally entitled the *Tractatus de summis pontificibus*. This work is first mentioned in Prior Peter's testimony on January 30, 1380 for the canonization commission set up by Pope Urban VI:[4]

> multe [sc. reuelaciones] continentur in libro celesti et multe in libro celesti jmperatoris ad reges et multe in tractatu de summis pontificibus

Thus, we learn that many revelations by Bridget are collected in the *Liber celestis*, many in the *Liber celestis imperatoris ad reges* and

---

[1] Bishop Alfonso has attracted considerable scholarly attention the past few years. See works by Aili, Gilkær, Sensi and the present writer in the bibliography.
[2] For the scholarly discussion of the process of codification of St. Bridget's revelations, see Jönsson, *Alfonso of Jaén*, pp. 85-108 with references.
[3] Klockars, *Birgitta och böckerna*, p. 332.
[4] *A & P*, p. 524.

14

many in the *Tractatus de summis pontificibus*. It is the last-mentioned collection, the last, shortest and most neglected one, that will be the subject of the present study.

In the printed editions of Bridget's *Revelaciones*, including the modern text critical one by Hans Aili, the revelations concerning the popes are to be found (together with some other revelations, about priests) at the end of book IV as chapters 132-144 under the joint title *Tractatus reuelacionum beate Birgitte ad sacerdotes et ad summos pontifices* ("Blessed Bridget's revelations to priests and popes"). However, a quick glance in Aili's *apparatus criticus* shows that this title has no manuscript authority, and there is, thus, no reason to believe that this arrangement was the original. In fact, the actual wording of the rubric to ch. 136[5] and readings reported in Aili's *apparatus criticus* clearly indicate that this part of book IV, viz. chs. 136-144,[6] originally constituted a separate work, and it has often been taken for granted that these nine revelations represented Alfonso's *Tractatus de summis pontificibus*.

1.3. Previous scholarly work on the *Tractatus*

In his pioneer work on the textual history of St. Bridget's revelations, *Några anmärkningar om Birgittas revelationer* ("Some remarks on Bridget's revelations"; Stockholm 1901)—a short, but very ingenious study—the great scholar Henrik Schück devotes some attention also to the *Tractatus de summis pontificibus* (pp. 21 and 24). He is the first in a succession of modern scholars who touches upon questions such as what was the content of Alfonso's original *Tractatus*, why was it compiled and why did Alfonso not include it in the *corpus reuelacionum* ("the collected works"). In Schück's opinion, Alfonso had tried to rearrange all the revelations that had been handed over to him in a thematical way, and in the *Tractatus* he had "included all or most of Bridget's attacks on the popes" (my translation). However according to Schück, this book had been considered unsuitable for publication at a time when Bridget's canonization was in the balance. These views are in the main subscribed to by recent scholars: for instance, Tore Nyberg, too, claims that Alfonso prepared thematical digests of the huge original collection of revelations with various addressees in mind and that the tractatus is such a collection addressed to "pontiffs and bish-

---

[5]*Reuelaciones infrascriptas habuit in visione spirituali Sancta Birgitta stando in oracione, que diriguntur ad summos pontifices innocentium vi, Urbanum v, gregorium xi...*

[6]Aili reports that one good manuscript explicitly gives the title *de summis pontificibus* to this part of book IV and in another one there is a marginal note reading: *Sequitur tractatus reuelacionum b.b. de summis pontificibus...*

ops",[7] and as concerns the question of why the *Tractatus* was not included in the *corpus reuelacionum*, Carl-Gustaf Undhagen, who dates the so-called second Alfonso redaction of the revelations (which did not include the *Tractatus*) to "around 1380",[8] concurs with Schück's opinion and writes that the omission was due to "ecclesiastical precaution".[9] As far as the content is concerned, Schück had maintained that the original *Tractatus* contained far more revelations than the nine in the printed editions, namely 57, as in book IX of the codex Harleyanus 612 in the British Museum (see my bibliography). Many other hypotheses as to the contents of this text have been put forward during the years: it has been suggested that it originally contained nine (as in the Ghotan edition), eleven, twelve, thirteen (as in various manuscripts of the *corpus reuelacionum*), twenty-one (as in a Florence manuscript; see below) or fifty-seven revelations (as in a British Library manuscript; see below).[10] The latest scholar to have expressed an opinion in this issue, Tore Nyberg,[11] subscribes to the fifty-seven-revelations-hypothesis originally propounded by Schück and further elaborated upon by Eric Colledge in his very influential article on Alfonso.[12]

In his edition of book IV (including the *Tractatus* part) published in 1992, Aili states, to be sure, that his aim is "to present the text of the original Alfonsine version". However, in actual fact he complies with the principles laid down by previous editors: namely, to stick to the *editio princeps*, the Ghotan edition, Lübeck 1492, as regards the *selection* and *arrangement* of the revelations, which, generally speaking, means that supplementary material (the *addiciones* and *declaraciones*) is interspersed between the chapters of the books of revelations as was the case in the Ghotan edition, even if this does not correspond to the original arrangement of either the first or the second Alfonsine edition. The *Tractatus* revelations, too, are presented by Aili in accordance with Ghotan: i. e. as chs. 136-144 of book IV, and the original title of the entire *Tractatus* (see p. 63) is retained as the heading of one single chapter, *viz.* ch. 136. However, in one respect Aili's arrangement is unprecedented: rev. VI: 63 is presented as *pars prior* of IV: 136.

---

[7]Nyberg, *Birgitta of Sweden*, pp. 38-39
[8]Undhagen, *Rev. I*, p. 24.
[9]Undhagen, *Rev. I*, p. 25.
[10]Undhagen, *Rev. I*, pp. 23-24, n. 93
[11] *Birgitta of Sweden*, p. 39.
[12]'Epistola solitarii', p. 33.

1.4. The aim of the present study

A number of hypotheses have been put forward as regards the content and arrangement of the *Tractatus*, but no systematic evaluation of the source manuscripts has been made and no edition has been presented that reconstructs the original Alfonsine version. The fundamental task will thus be to present such an edition.

A supplementary reason for making a reappraisal of the text is that there are some puzzling readings in the recent edition: e. g., which are the "undecim verba" spoken to Pope Gregory (IV: 142: 4), how can the pope be requested to bend the "*cardines* ad velle suum" and forbid them, the *cardines*, to have more clothes, servants, etc, than they really need? (IV: 49: 17, cf. below rev. III: 17), how are we to understand the enlarged rubric to IV: 144, reported in the *apparatus criticus*, that seems to imply that the pope in question is Gregory XI, and what about the dating of IV: 141? Are the words *in festo Sancti Policarpi* really an interpolation?

On the basis of the reconstructed text, I will then make a reappraisal of the following, much discussed questions: what was the title and content of the original *Tractatus*? When was it compiled and for what purpose? Why was it omitted in the early editions? To what extent did Alfonso revise St. Bridget's revelations?

2. The manuscripts of the *Tractatus* and their mutual relations

The manuscripts in which we find the so-called *Tractatus de summis pontificibus* can on the face of it be divided into two groups: the *corpus reuelacionum* manuscripts in which we find the *Tractatus* as a sequel to book IV (below ch. 2.1) and those manuscripts where the *Tractatus* is handed down separately (below chs. 2.2 and 2.5).

2.1. The *corpus reuelacionum* tradition

2.1.1. The selection of manuscripts

St. Bridget's books of revelations are preserved in a considerable number of manuscripts. The editors of the modern critical editions of the various books of the *Liber celestis* have divided the extant manuscripts into two main groups, the β-group and the π-group, the main difference being that in the manuscripts of the latter group, there is some supplementary material (including the *Tractatus*) that the β-manuscripts lack.[13] The fact that the *Tractatus* is not to be found in the β-group means that this collection was not included in the redactions of the revelations Alfonso himself had made, the first of which had contained only books I-VII and the second of which had been enlarged to include *Epistola solitarii, Liber celestis imperatoris ad reges, Sermo Angelicus* and, probably, *Quatuor Oraciones*. For the reconstruction of the *Tractatus* text of the π-hyparchetype, the following four manuscripts, *viz.* **y**, **q**, **K** and **F**, have been selected on the basis of previous investigations by Bergh, Undhagen and Aili[14] for their respective editions of the books of the *Liber celestis*:

y = *Prague*, Universitní Knihovna, ms. V. G. 20, late 14th century, ff. 167r-174v.

q = *Vienna*, Nationalbibliothek, ms. 3960, 1380-1386, ff. 158r-160v.

F = *Lund*, The University Library, ms. 21 ("Codex Falkenberg"), late 14th century, ff. 171vb-177ra.[15]

K = *Kalmar*, Stifts- och Gymnasiebiblioteket (deposited in Lund University Library), late 14th century, ff. 109rb-112va.

---

[13]Undhagen, *Rev. I*, p. 52.

[14]See the bibliography, particularly Undhagen, *Rev. I*, p. 228.

[15]Edited in facsimile by E. Wessén, see Birgitta, *Revelationes*

In the selected manuscripts of the *corpus reuelacionum*, the *Tractatus* is copied as a sequel to book IV. The manuscripts differ a little as to the selection and arrangement of the revelations included in the *Tractatus* part. In the table below, I give a survey of the contents of the *Tractatus* in the these manuscripts. (In the interest of clarity, I have also included in this table corresponding information for the other manuscripts I have investigated, below pp. 30-33 and 23-25.) The revelations for which there is evidence in the manuscripts have been numbered by me consecutively as I-XIII, and in the respective columns, I have indicated the content of the various manuscripts and also whether the revelations are written out in full or truncated. Their numbers in the printed editions are stated, too, in order to facilitate identification.

My numbers[17]	Gh[16]	Corpus reuelacionum mss.				Other manuscripts.			
		y	q	K	F	L	p	Z^a	W^b
Rev. I	(VI:63)	x	(x)	x	x	x	x	x	x
II	IV:136	x	x	x	x	x	x	x	x
III	(IV:49)	(*x*)	(*x*)	(*x*)	(*x*)	x	x	x	x
IV	IV:137	x	x	x	x	x	x	x	x
V	IV:138	x	x	x	x	x	x	x[18]	x
VI	IV:139	x	x	x	x	x	x		x
VII	IV:140	x	x	x	x	x	x		x
VIII	IV:141	x	x	x	x	x	x		x
IX	IV:142	x	x	x	x	x	x		x
X	IV:143	x	x	x	x	x	x		x
XI	(VII:31)	(x)	(x)	(x)	(*x*)	0	0		x
XII	(VI:96)	(x)	0	(x)	(*x*)	0	(x)		x
XIII	IV:144	x	x	x	x	x[19]	x		x[20]

x = revelation copied in its entirety
(x) = the beginning of the revelation is copied
(*x*) = revelation indicated in the margin
0 = revelation not copied

---

[16] In the *editio princeps* (**Gh**) and the other printed editions, those four revelations that had been taken over from the *Liber Celestis* were completely omitted and the remaining ones numbered consecutively, so from these it was impossible to deduce anything about the original content.

[17] In $Z^a W^b$ **yq KF**, the revelations of the *Tractatus* were *not* numbered originally; in **K**, however, they were numbered 136-148 by a second hand. In **p**, the extant revelations are numbered I-XII and in **L** 1-11.

[18] The manuscript is mutilated after § 14, *sua fraude*.

[19] After the 13th revelation, which is numbered as "Capitulum 11" in **L**, a *declaratio* is added. The remaining chapters (f. 125r-127r) contain supplementary material, most of which belongs to the group known as the *reuelaciones extrauagantes*, see Hollman, p. 55. (Chapter 49, not identified by Hollman, corresponds to Rev. VI: 120: 5.)

[20] Another eight revelations follow, see below pp. 24-25.

There is, thus, evidence for thirteen revelations in the *corpus revela-cionum* tradition of the *Tractatus*. However, as is shown above, four of the thirteen revelations are duplicates of revelations in the *Liber cel-estis*, a fact that was realized by those who copied the *Tractatus* as part of the *corpus reuelacionum*. It was obviously considered unneces-sary to write the same revelations more than once. Judging from the manuscripts (see the table above), it can be assumed that the hyp-archetype of the π-group was arranged in the following way: the first revelation of the *Tractatus*, which had already been edited as VI: 63, was copied in full, but the other three duplicate revelations were trun-cated (only the chapter heading and the first words of the revelations proper were copied). For the full text, the reader was referred to cor-responding revelations in the *Liber celestis*. In the manuscripts, the duplicate revelations of the *Tractatus* are thus treated in a fairly con-sistent way—unlike the duplicate revelations of the *Liber celestis im-peratoris ad reges,* which sometimes was written out in full in the *Li-ber celestis* and truncated in the *Liber celestis imperatoris ad reges* and sometimes copied the other way round.[21] The reason for this is, of course, that the *Tractatus* was added to the *corpus revelationum* at a later stage than the *Liber celestis imperatoris ad reges*, when the pro-cess of codification was already finished and the copyist, or perhaps rather the promotor, of the copy that was to become known to scholars of our days as the π-hyparchetype had already arranged it in an ap-propriate way.

2.1.2. The relationship between yq and KF

There are a number of passages where **y** and **q** have one reading and **K** and **F** another, as for instance in the following cases:

	y q	K F
I R	de regno suecie ordinis cisterciensis	cisterciencis ordinis de regno suecie
IV R	beate b(irgitte)	beate virginis in watz-steno
VI:5	deficeret...eleuauit...fouit... calefecit...cibauit	deficiat...eleuat...fouet... calefacit...cibat
VII:7	aliqui	alii
VIII:2	frigus	frigor
IX R	Hec...MCCCLXXIII	Reuelacio...Gregorio
IX:3	qui	que
IX:5	celestem curiam meam	curiam meam celestem

---

[21]Aili, *Rev. IV*, pp. 43-45.

	y q	**K F**
IX:19	rapiat	rapiet
X R	domina	beata
XIII:1	astabat	stabat
XIII:7	licitum est	est licitum

As a rule, it is not easy to tell which reading is wrong, but some cases merit closer consideration, and I believe that some common errors can be suspected for both **K** and **F** on the one hand and **y** and **q** on the other.

Possible errors in K and F:
In VIII: 2, **K F** give the reading *frigor*, whereas **y q** have *frigus*. To be sure, *frigor* does exist, but since it is otherwise unknown in the *Reuelaciones*, we can undoubtedly regard it is an error in this case.

In rev. X R, it is obvious that *domina* is the original reading and that *beata* is a modernisation in **K F** (as well as in III R **K**), but it is not necessary that it indicates a common source, since this alteration could easily have been induced separately. (I can here anticipate the results of my investigation and mention as another example that the **K F** reading in IV R *beate virginis in watzsteno* is unauthentic as well.) **K F** (or perhaps rather a common source) have thus been the object of a deliberate—albeit gentle—revision.

As regards the series of readings in VI: 5, cf. below pp. 36-39.

Possible errors in y and q
In IX: 3 *que* may be the correct reading (*que tres persone unum sumus in diuinitatis substancia*, 'for we three persons are one in the substance of the Godhead'). The reading *qui* may have arisen due to the antecedent *(Pater et) Spiritus Sanctus.*

In IX: 19 the subjunctive *rapiat* is probably wrong. The future tense *rapiet* of **K F** is supported by the same tense in the other verbs *faciam...deponam ..erunt...repleberis* (IX: 18-19).

Unlike some of those in **K F**, the possible errors in **y q** must be classified as slips of the pen.

On the basis of the variant readings reported above, it is feasible to divide these manuscripts into two groups in the *stemma codicum*, namely **y q** and **K F** respectively. To be sure, this result is quite surprising in view of Aili's conclusion that **K** and **F** belong to two different subgroups and, consequently, that whenever "**K** and **F** agree, they ... give the text of the archetype,"[22] but as far as I can understand, Aili has not pin-pointed any shared errors for **K** and **F** in chapters 136-144 (=

---

[22] Aili, *Rev. IV*, p. 42.

the *Tractatus*) specifically. On the other hand, my conclusions square well with the results obtained by Bergh and Undhagen in their investigations of the supplementary material in books VII and I respectively: in their editions, **K** and **F** belong to one branch of a bipartite stemma and **q** the other.[23] (Neither Bergh nor Undhagen uses **y** for their editions.)

The duplicate, first revelation.

Since the first revelation of the *Tractatus*, which was taken over from the *Liber celestis*, VI: 63, is written out in full in **y**, **K** and **F**, I have also compared variant readings in these two editions of the same revelation. (As for **q**, only the chapter heading and a few initial words were copied.) Fortunately, we have book VI in a recent text-critical edition by Bergh, and in my comparison I assume quite simply that he has managed to reconstruct Alfonso's original and that this is the text Alfonso had before him when compiling the *Tractatus*.

	VI: 63 (ed. Bergh)	**Tractatus, rev. I** (see below p. 39-40)
R	Christus dat ... Cap. LXIII	Christus per ... ordinis Cisterciensis
§ 1	Filius loquitur ad sponsam	Filius Dei loquitur ad sponsam dicens **y q K F**
	hec verba	verba hec **q K F** hec verba **y**
	super	per **y q K F**
§ 2	in	ad **y K F**
	vide	videas **y** vide **K F**
§ 3	ad	*om.* **y K F**
	iudicans	iudicans **y** audiens **K F**
§ 5	quam[1]	quod **y** quam **K F**
	melius ego Deus	melius ego deus **y**
		ego deus melius **K F**
§ 6	tempore tuo floruit	tempore tuo floruit **y**
		floruit tempore tuo **K F**
§ 8	quoque	enim **y K F**

Thus, in the *Tractatus* the rubric has been thoroughly revised; specific facts as to the date of the revelation and as to who transmitted Bridget's message to the pope have been added. Alfonso gives the same information in his *Informaciones* (§ 3-10).

In § 1, *Filius* has been made clearer by the addition of *Dei*. It is obviously motivated by the desire to be more precise about who the son is, since the revelation comes first in the new collection.

---

[23]Bergh, *Rev. VII*, pp. 70-76 and Undhagen, *Rev. I*, p. 224.

As far as the other cases are concerned where the *Tractatus* manuscripts offers another reading than book VI, it is difficult to tell whether the variants are revisions by the editor or simple slips of the copyist's pen.

In one case, however, it is quite possible that the *Tractatus* has preserved the authentic reading and that we thus can detect an archetypal error in book VI. The case I have in mind is § 1 *super/per*. I am tempted to regard the *Tractatus* reading *per omnes gradus* as the correct reading on the strength of the parallel passage in § 4, where both book VI and the *Tractatus* have this reading (For another example, see VIII: 4: 1: *Dixi regi prius quosdam gradus*, per *quos as-cendere potest ad celestia*). The reading *super* may have arisen under the influence of the following *surge*. If so, this confirms Bergh's conclusion that the archetype was not identical with Alfonso's original.[24]

Of particular interest are the cases where only **y** or only **K F** offer another reading than the one we find in the revelation in book VI. In two cases, **y** offers distinctive variant readings (§ 2 *videas*, § 5 *quod*) and, similarly, **K** and **F** in three cases (§ 3 *audiens*, § 5 *ego deus melius*, § 6 *floruit tempore tuo*). It is feasible to regard these deviations from the original as errors which confirm the classification and evaluation of the manuscripts made above solely on internal criteria.

2.2. The **Zᵃ** and **Wᵇ** manuscripts

As mentioned above, Aili's edition of the *Tractatus* is based entirely on manuscripts of the *corpus reuelacionum* tradition. There are, however, other manuscripts as well that contain versions of the *Tractatus* and should be considered for the establishment of this text (see the table p. 19). Here I will discuss two of these, namely the following:

Zᵃ = *Helsinki*, University Library, "Codex Nordenskiöld", early 15th century, ff. 117v-120.[25]

Wᵇ = *Florence*, Biblioteca Medicea Laurenziana, ms. Ashb. 896, a paper-booklet, early 15th century, ff. 1-19r.[26]

These manuscripts can be dated to the early 15th century on paleographical grounds. Both of them have a very interesting provenience.

---

[24]Bergh, *Rev. VI*, p. 26.
[25]For a detailed description of the manuscript, see Jörgensen.
[26]Described by Ekwall, *Vår äldsta Birgittavita*, p. 38 (figure 7).

In **Z**^a (f. 115r) there is a note in the margin of Rev. ex. 49 (one of those revelations in which Alfonso was commissioned editor), which reads as follows (to be sure, in a somewhat peculiar Latin):[27]

> Hec revelatio causa humilitatis idem episcopus non adscripsit in libro reuelationum. Sed ego scriptor reperj eam in suo breuiario post mortem suam elapsit aliquibus annijs M°CCCC°

We learn thus that out of humility the bishop had not included this revelation in the book of revelations, but "I, the scribe, found it in his breviary some years after his death, in the year 1400." To be sure, the note in **Z**^a is hardly original, but copied (together with the revelation itself) from the source manuscript, but in this way we learn at least that the scribe of that manuscript must have worked in the convent San Girolamo di Quarto in Genoa where Alfonso had died in 1389. We know from another source, too—Alfonso's *Conscripcio de eleccione Urbani sexti* (p. 97)—that the bishop had his private papers in Genoa.

That the other manuscript, as well, **W**^b, is related in some way to this monastery is learned from a letter, f. 18r-18v, which is subscribed:

> Janue in Monasterio nostro S[anct]i Jeronimi di Quarto Riperie diocesis Januensis M°CCCC°II°

On the strength of this subscription, Sara Ekwall dated the manuscript to 1402, but I do not believe that this letter is in the original, because the name of the sender is omitted and replaced with three dots: *Et ego frater ... conscriptor et miniator harum reuelationum humilis monachus ordinis montisoliueti,* an arrangement difficult to understand if we take the letter to be an original. The name of the addressee is missing, but he was, according to the sender, known for his devotion to God, Christ and Bridget.

W^b is unique in that it has preserved all the above-traced 13 revelations of the *Tractatus* written out in full. After them follow eight others with roughly similar contents: the so-called simony office,[28] revelations VI 74 and 70, IV 33, 10, 5 (extract), 57 and 78, the above-

---

[27] Jörgensen, p. 56, cf. Hollman, p. 97.

[28] It is a spirited attack on the vice of simony ("de horrore symonie procacis"). In a vision Bridget sees that the house of Simon Magus "alcius creuerat quam predicta ecclesia sancte crucis [in roma]." Like the *Tractatus*, the simony office had not been included in the *corpus reuelacionum*, but had been found among the papers Alfonso left behind. "The Spaniard Alfonso" had been entrusted with the task of presenting it to the pope (Urban V or Gregory XI).

In modern times the text has been printed three times, but from another manuscript, C 86 in Uppsala University Library, the only one known to these scholars (Schück, pp. 55-56; Westman, pp. 293-295 and Schmid, pp. 203-206).

mentioned letter, and finally, on page 19r, another hand has copied a revelation to Giovanni dalle Celle.[29]

It was once suggested by Ekwall that this manuscript represented an original twenty-one-revelations-version of the *Tractatus*,[30] but, as I have previously argued, this is hardly the case.[31] Rather we have here another example of the thirteen-revelations-version, to which some other revelations have been added. In the manuscript, there is, to be sure, a line after rev. XIII, but it of course impossible to draw any conclusions from that. My arguments for making a distinction between the first 13 revelations and the following eight are instead based on the following facts:

1. In the first part of the manuscript, from f. 1ᵛ to f. 11ʳ, there are page rubrics. We read REUELACIONES AD on the upper left-hand page and SUMMOS PONTIFICES on the upper right-hand page. The last place where these page rubrics are found is on top of the pages where the thirteenth revelation is found. After that there are no page rubrics at all. This omission is easily explained if we assume that the copyist—or his source—knew that the rest of the revelations were *not* part of the *Tractatus*.

2. A look at the supplementary revelations show for instance that in the chapter heading of revelation VI: 74, Bridget is referred to as *beata*. Thus we read *Videbat sponsa Christi beata Brigida,* etc. But in the title of the *Tractatus*, as well as in III R and VIII R, Bridget is referred to as *domina* Brigida, not *beata* Brigida. This inconsistency is explained if these last revelations did not belong to Alfonso's collection of revelations.

3. Among the first 13 chapters, there are four taken from books IV, VI and VII of the *Liber celestis*, but there are no references to this source. The last seven revelations are *all* taken from books IV and VI of the *Liber celestis*. In all these cases there are explicit references to the corresponding book and revelation in the *Liber celestis*. This inconsistency in the way of referring to the revelations quoted is easily explained if we assume that the last eight revelations did not belong to the original *Tractatus* collection.

On the strength of these observations I thus conclude that in this manuscript we have a copy of the *Tractatus* with its 13 revelations *and* another eight revelations, collected by someone interested in having other thematically related revelations conveniently added to the *Tractatus*.

---

[29]Published in Ekwall, 'Quando morì'. On Giovanni and his interests in pope prophesies, see Grundmann, pp. 34-36

[30]*Vår äldsta Birgittavita*, p. 37 n. 24 and p. 38.

[31]Jönsson, 'On the so-called *Tractatus*', pp. 22-23.

2.3. The relationship between the *corpus reuelacionum* and the Z^a W^b manuscripts.

A question of prime importance now has to be solved: was the *Tractatus* text of the Florence and Helsinki manuscripts copied from *corpus reuelacionum* manuscripts, or does it derive independently from Alfonso's original? In the former case, these manuscripts are not particularly important for the establishment of the genuine Alfonsine text; in the later, they are very important, since this would mean that we have access to sources that are independent of the *corpus reuelacionum* tradition.

For the classification of the Z^a and W^b manuscripts in relation to the *corpus revelacionum* manuscripts, there are a number of interesting variant readings to examine:

	$Z^a W^b$	yq KF
Title	brigida	birgitta **q KF** b y
I R	dedit	dat
I R	clementi sexto	clementi quinto
I R	et veniret	et quod veniret
I:2	in ytaliam	ad ytaliam*
I:6	*om.*	regum*
I:8	*om.*	tua*
IV:1	glomationem	glomeracionem
IV:1	defilare	filare
IV:1	*om.*	utitur
V:6	accurrente Z^a accurrere W^b	occurrentem
VII: 13	peccatis W^b	penis **y q**
		prauis operibus **K F**

In some cases there is no difficulty in evaluating the alternatives: for example, it seems quite obvious that the authentic form (i.e. the form used by Alfonso) of the saint's name is *Brigida*, not *Birgitta*,[32] that the pope mentioned in I R is Clement VI (pope 1342-52), not Clement V (pope 1305-14), and that *in Ytaliam*, not *ad Ytaliam* is the reading of the original (cf. VI: 63, as reconstructed by Birger Bergh). Thus, in these cases the Z^a W^b readings are in all probability authentic.

In VII: 13 the manuscripts offer three different readings, two of which, *peccatis* and *prauis operibus*, are acceptable from the point of

---

*These readings are to be found only in **y KF**, since the revelation itself was not written out in **q** (see the table p. 19).

[32]Jönsson, *Alfonso of Jaén*, p. 113, n. 4 and p. 185 (Alfonso's *Informaciones*, § 3, 8, 9, etc.

view of context, whereas the third, *penis*, does not make good sense and cannot reasonably be authentic. This distribution of readings can be explained by assuming that *peccatis* is the original reading. If this word was written in an abbreviated form, as it is most often, it may have been misread as *penis*,[33] which thus may have been the reading of the p-hyparchetype, preserved in **yq**. If these suppositions are correct, the **KF** reading must be regarded as an attempt by some copyist to correct the impossible reading *penis*. It may be added that the phrase *praua opera* is most unusual in the *Reuelaciones,* where the normal expression is *mala opera.*

On the other hand, there are a number of cases where it can be concluded with reasonable certainty that the **yq KF** readings are to be preferred and that, thus, the **Z^{a}W^b** readings are to be considered as errors:

In I R the present *dat* is obviously correct in view of the following *precipit*, also in the present tense, with which it is coordinated, and also in view of the fact that this is the reading in the chapter heading of rev. VI: 63 (*Christus dat sponse* etc).

In the choice between *et veniret* and *et quod veniret* in I R, it seems safe to prefer the latter, since this is the variant supported by the corresponding passage in VI: 63. For the same reason, *regum* (I: 6) and *tua* (I: 8) must be considered authentic in the *Tractatus* text.

As for *defilare* (IV: 1), I suppose that this reading is due to influence from the preceding *desinit* and that thus *filare* is authentic.

A most interesting case is V: 6. There are two grammatically possible variants, viz. *accurrere* **W^b** and *occurrentem* **yq KF**, but since **W^b** was probably copied from **Z^a** (p. 30), *accurrere* is hardly a possible choice stemmatically. It can be explained as an attempt to correct the impossible **Z^a** reading *occurrente*, obviously caused by the omission of the nasal stroke for the final *m*.

On the strength of these observations it seems reasonable to conclude that neither is the **Z^a W^b** text derived from the *corpus reuelacionum* text nor vice versa.

The duplicate revelations
What about the status of the duplicate revelations that are written out in full in **Z^a W^b**, but truncated in the *corpus reuelacionum* manuscripts: do the third, eleventh and twelfth revelations in **Z^a W^b** derive their origin from a manuscript that contained the text of all thirteen revelations of Alfonso's original *Tractatus* or had they been omitted there and was added by the copyists of **Z^a W^b** directly from IV: 49, VII: 31 and VI: 96, respectively?

---

[33]On the problem of undiscovered abbreviations, see Bergh, *Palaeography*, pp. 17-23.

To answer this question, some variant readings must be examined (I give a somewhat simplified report):[34]

IV:49   **Tractatus, rev. III (Z^a)**

	IV:49	Tractatus, rev. III (Z^a)
§ 4	debent PY^1 β_2 deberent Y^2V π	debent
§ 11	custodiuntur et possidentur PY^1 custodiuntur *cet.*	custodiuntur et possidentur
§ 19	eos (*post* abhominantur) π *om.* β	*om.*

	VII:31	rev. XI (W^b)
§§ 4, 6, 9	*see below*	*see below*
§ 7	et complebuntur omnia illa, que dicta sunt tibi π *om.* β	et complebuntur omnia illa, que dicta sunt

	VI:96	rev. XII (W^b)
§ 5	salutem β requiem P π	requiem

The fact that the *Tractatus* readings correspond to β-readings in IV: 49 does not prove, of course, that it is derived from a separate *Tractatus* version, since irrespective of whether the Z^a text comes directly from IV: 49 or indirectly via the *Tractatus*, we are entitled to expect that the ultimate source is of the β-type. However, a most interesting fact is that rev. XI: 7 presents a reading that does not belong to the β-group, but to the π-group, which cannot possibly have been available in Italy at that time. How are we to explain that? I would suggest that the reason is that this revelation was *not* copied from a *corpus reuelacionum* manuscript, but from a separate *Tractatus* manuscript that certainly contained rev. XI and perhaps all thirteen revelations.

In III: 11, the Z^a reading corresponds to a variant that in all probability was not the reading of the archetype. Obviously, in 1379, Alfonso copied from a text that was not the original.

As regards the eleventh revelation in general, there are important differences between it and the corresponding revelation in book VII. Let us, however, first take a look at the rubrics to the two versions:

> Rev. VII: 31 (ed. Bergh): *Christus in Roma loquens sponse sue beate Birgitte predicit ei diem et modum mortis sue, ordinans, quid fiat de libris reuelacionum. Dicit eciam, quod multi erunt in mundo, qui illas recipi-*

---

[34]I refer the reader to Aili's and Bergh's editions (*cet.* = *ceteri codices ab Ailio adhibiti*) for detailed information about the manuscript tradition.

ent cum deuocione, quando ei placuerit, qui optinebunt graciam eius. Disponit eciam Dominus de corpore sponse sue, vbi debeat sepeliri. Cap. XXXI.

and

Tractatus de summis pontificibus, rev. 11: *Paulo ante mortem habuit sponsa Christi subscriptam reuelacionem a Christo, que tangit dictum dominum papam Gregorium super aduentum ad Romam.*

In the rubric originally written for this revelation in book VII, we learn that Christ predicts Bridget's death and gives instructions about the editing of the books of revelations. The Lord adds that many people will receive the revelations with devotion and finally gives instructions about Bridget's burial. In the *Tractatus*, we learn that it is a revelation about Pope Gregory's return to Rome. This wording squares well with the general content of the *Tractatus*, but has nothing in common with the rubric in book VII. A comparison of the two versions of this revelation shows that in the *Tractatus* we have a somewhat abbreviated version of the corresponding revelation in book VII: § 4 is cut after the word *paratum,* § 6 is truncated, too, and § 9 is entirely omitted. A clear tendency is noticeable: in §§ 6 and 9 there are instructions about Alfonso's editing of the revelations. These passages were not only totally irrelevant in a work that aimed at proving that it was God's will that the popes reside in Rome, but in fact a mentioning of Alfonso's rôle as editor might compromise the credibility of the message. The combined evidence of the rubric and the deletions gives us reason to believe that the version of rev. XI, as preserved in the Florence manuscript, is the result of a deliberate adaptation of VII: 31 to the new context, not scribal neglect or carelessness. If I am right here, it is thanks to the Florence manuscript—which, as mentioned above, is the only manuscript that has rev. XI written out in full—that we get this glimpse into Alfonso's workshop.

We notice that in the *Tractatus*, as in book VII as well, the chapter headings give supplementary information about why, when or where St. Bridget had the revelations in question (and that in the past tense). Otherwise the chapter heading merely summmarizes the content of the revelation (in the present tense). It is most illustrative in this respect to compare the chapter heading of IV: 49:

Visio sponse sub figura Ecclesie; et de eius exposicione, in qua continentur modus et status, quos Papa debet tenere respectu sui et respectu cardinalium et aliorum prelatorum sancte matris Ecclesie, et quam maxime in statu humilitatis.

and the *Tractatus*, rev. III:

> Una die antequam papa Urbanus V intraret Romam, habuit domina
> Brigida infrascriptam reuelacionem in Sancta Maria Maiori in Roma,
> que tractat de reparacione Ecclesie.

These two rubrics refer in actual fact to the very same revelation, but are written for two different contexts.

W[b] is also the only manuscript that preserves the chapter heading of rev. XII. In the other manuscripts, in which there is a reference to this revelation, the chapter heading is omitted and the place of the revelation is indicated with the initial words "Paulo ante mortem", etc. Curiously enough, in **y**, this heading is preserved as the heading of rev. XIII, whose original heading was displaced, probably because of the similarity in wording.

2.4. The relationship between the Z^a and W^b manuscripts

As to the relative worth of the Florence and Helsinki manuscripts, it can easily be demonstrated that the latter manuscript is marred by a great number of individual errors, e. g., III: 9 Respondi **W**[b], Respondit *ceteri*; III: 9 Exponet **W**[b], Expone *ceteri*; III: 18 Qi **W**[b], Qui *ceteri*. Nothing similar can be shown for **Z**[a]. In fact, it is quite possible, as far as I can see, that **W**[b] was copied from **Z**[a]. As mentioned above, **Z**[a] is mutilated, and must therefore, regrettably, be replaced with **W**[b] for the missing part.

2.5. The L and p manuscripts

As shown in the table above, p. 19, the *Tractatus* is preserved also in the Vadstena manuscript **p** (ff. 54v-59r) and in the Syon Abbey manuscript **L** (ff. 125ra-127rb). In **L**, the books of the *Liber Celestis* were copied from a β-manuscript,[35] which thus means that the supplementary revelations (including the *Tractatus*) were missing. Some of that material (including the *Tractatus*) was collected and edited in a ninth book, which begins: *Incipit liber nonus celestium reuelacionum qui intitulatur ad pontifices et continet multas alias reuelaciones que non agunt de pontificibus vt patebit.* In spite of this incipit, which explicitly states that the book contains the *liber ad pontifices*[36] as well as many other revelations that are not about popes, it has surprisingly

---

[35]Undhagen, *Rev. I*, p. 199.
[36]For this alternative designation to *Tractatus de summis pontificibus*, see below p. 63.

enough been suggested, as mentioned above, p. 16, that book nine in its entirety represented the Alfonsine *Tractatus*.

The **p** and **L** manuscripts have been discussed by previous editors of the revelations. Lennart Hollman, who analyses these manuscripts (**p** was then designated **v**) in his edition of the *Reuelaciones extrauagantes*, concludes that, compared to **K** and **F**, they are of secondary importance as sources to the original text.[37] Bergh analyses the place of these manuscripts in the textual tradition for the supplementary material to Book VII and advances the following stemma (p. 112):

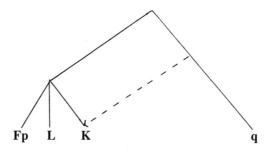

As far as the *Tractatus* is concerned, it can easily be demonstrated that in this case, too, the text in **p** and **L** is closely related to that of the Vadstena manuscripts **K** and **F** and to the *editio princeps*, **Gh**.

Some **K F** errors were pin-pointed in rev. I (above p. 23). These errors are shared by **p** and/or **L** as follows:

| § 5 | ego deus melius | **KF** and **pL** |
| § 6 | floruit tempore tuo | **KF** and **p** |

As far as the other possible errors in **K** and **F** are concerned (see above), the manipulation of *domina* into *beata* is shared by **p** and **L**. The passage VI: 5-6 is particularly interesting: above, I assumed that *currit* was an error that in **K** and **F** had caused emendation of the following verbs to obtain consistency in the use of tenses. In **L** *currit* has been changed instead, to *occurrit*, an emendation that is consistent with the perfect of the following verbs.

Another illustrative passage is V:2 *Quamuis infantes habeant suam necessitatem (suam necessitatem* om. **K** *gaudium* **Fp**) *secundum suam voluntatem*... The other manuscripts retained *suam necessitatem*. This distribution of variants indicates that these words were omitted in the source of **KFp** and that *gaudium* is an emendation in **Fp** (induced by *gaudium* in the following sentence) to supply *habeant* with a badly needed object.

---

[37]Hollman, p. 49 and 61-62.

The duplicate revelations

In **p** and **L**, but not in **K F** and in **y q**, rev. III is copied in its entirety. This is potentially a significant difference. As was the case with **Z**[a] and **W**[b], the occurrence of the full text can in principle be explained in either of two ways: the revelation was copied from a manuscript of the *Tractatus*, in which it was written out in full—in this case the stemma has to be thoroughly revised—or the copyist completed his text by recourse directly to book IV: 49. In the former case, the manuscripts would, of course, be of immense importance for an edition of the *Tractatus*, since they would be a source for rev. III and represent another branch of the *Tractatus* tradition; in the latter case, they are not very important, since it is not book IV we are editing.

To illustrate this question, I will here quote some variant readings from rev. III and compare them with variant readings in IV:49:

IV:49 (ed. Aili)[38]   **Tractatus, rev. III**

§ 17 de familia α et familia **F Gh**   et fam. **p L** de fam. **Z**[a] **W**[b]

§ 10 similatur et designatur α   des. et sim. **p**
     des. et sim. **F**   sim. et des. **Z**[a] **W**[b]
§ 18 flectantur α flectentur **KF**   flectentur **p** flectantur **Z**[a] **W**[b]

§ 15 quod α ut **G h**   vt **L** quod **Z**[a] **W**[b]
§ 17 usus vite α vite usus **Gh**   vite usus **L** usus vite **Z**[a] **W**[b]
§ 20 emendare potest papa in mul-   papa in m. e. potest **L**
     tis α papa in m. e. potest **G h**   e. potest papa in m. **Z**[a] **W**[b]
§ 20 necessaria α necessaria sua **K**   necessaria sua **L**
                                            necessaria **Z**[a] **W**[b]
§ 21 quicumque α qui **G h**   qui **L** quicumque **Z**[a] **W**[b]

Thus, we find that **K F Gh** errors in IV: 49 are found in the *Tractatus* text of **p** and **L** as well: **p** shares errors with **F**, and **L** with **K**. It seems reasonable to assume that rev. III was copied from IV: 49, since it was missing in the source. (It is interesting to note that **L** shares some errors with **Gh**, which are not to be found in **K** and **F**. These errors must have existed in a source manuscript older than **L**. Thus, **K** and **F** cannot have been the only source of **Gh**.)

---

[38]I quote only the archetype (= α, as reconstructed by Aili, *Rev. IV*, pp. 164-166) and the **KF Gh** readings. For a full report, I refer the reader to Aili's *apparatus criticus*. To be sure, a possible source of error is the principles adopted by Aili (and Bergh, *Rev. VI*) as regards the strict selection of readings reported in the *apparatus criticus*, but since the picture in the main is clear and my results are supported by what we know about the history of the manuscripts, I do not think that is a real problem.

As far as rev. I in **L** is concerned, there is a reading that positively gives us reason to suspect that the source of this revelation is not to be found in the *Tractatus* but in the *Liber Celestis*. In § 1 we read *super omnes gradus* with the latter branch of the tradition, not *per omnes gradus* as in the other *Tractatus* manuscripts (cf. above p. 23).

Evaluation of *p*

To be sure, **p** cannot have been copied—directly or indirectly—from **F**, since there is an omission in this manuscript, rev. X: 2, that has no parallel in **p**, but considering the fact that **p** in the main represents the same Vadstena recension of the *Tractatus* as **F**, as is demonstrated by a number of shared errors, i. e. V: 2 *gaudium*, see above, V: 9 *caritatem suam*, V: 13 *ego duxi*, VI: 1 *eius consciencia* and VI: 2 *illa tunc*, I find it unmotivated to use this manuscript for an edition of the *Tractatus*.

Evaluation of *L*

L seems to represent another twig on the Vadstena branch, and in a number of cases it offers—versus **KF**—the same reading as $(\mathbf{Z}^a)\mathbf{W}^b$ **yq**, in all probability the correct reading:

	$(\mathbf{Z}^a)\mathbf{W}^b$ **yq**	**KF**	**L**
II:1	suscipiendos, -um	recipiendum	suscipiendos
IV:7	dicte indulgencie	indulg. dicte	dicte indulg.
IV:8	tuum monasterium	monast. tuum	tuum monast.
V:5	periculis	periculo	periculis
V:6	viderit	videt	viderit
VI:1	eius corporis	corporis eius	eius corporis
VI:7	ego	*om.*	ego
IX:10	ipsarum	animarum	ipsarum
XIII:7	licitum est	est licitum	licitum est

On the other hand, **L** has been the object of deliberate revision: for instance, the original title has been replaced with a new incipit, the text of rev. III (and possibly of rev. I) is not the original (see above) and some chapter headings have been enlarged by short summaries of the contents. In addition, this manuscript has a considerable number of individual errors. (To give some idea about the frequency and character of these readings, I quote some examples from rev. II: R Clementem sextum **L** Clementem *ceteri*; medio eorum **L** medio *ceteri*; audierit **L** audiret *ceteri*.) For these reasons, I am of the opinion that it is not worthwhile to encumber the *apparatus criticus* with readings from this manuscript, and I have consequently not used **L** for my edition.

2.6. The stemma

The observations I have reported above can be accounted for by the following *stemma codicum*:

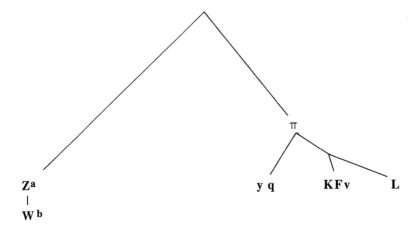

3. Principles of edition

3.1. The reconstruction of the archetype

Rev. I-II, IV-X and XIII

The archetype is reconstructed on the basis of a comparison between Z^a or (where this manuscript is mutilated) W^b on the one hand and the π-hyparchetype on the other. A reading extant in Z^a/W^b and in at least one of the two subgroups of the π-hyparchetype, i. e., in either **yq** or **KF**, must be considered to have already existed in the archetype.

In the cases where Z^a/W^b has one reading and π another and it does not seem possible to rule out either on contextual or linguistic grounds, I have preferred π, since this source seems to give a generally superior text. One type of difference between the two sources is that a certain word is found in π but not in Z^a/W^b. In most cases it is impossible to tell which is correct, but there are a few cases where it is reasonable to suspect that it is the question of omissions in Z^a/W^b, not additions in π: e. g. IV:1 *utitur* (obviously correct) and perhaps III:2 *suam*. Unfortunately, W^b in particular seems to be marred by errors. To give some idea of the character and frequency of these suspicious readings, I quote some examples from rev. XIII: § 1 the omission of *sponsa*, § 3 *audiuit* and *illa*, § 5 the omission of *in* and § 8 *quibus*.

In those cases too where Z^a/W^b has a reading in common with one of the other manuscripts, I have opted for this reading.

Rev. III, XI-XII (the duplicate revelations)

Since these revelations are not written out in the manuscripts of the *corpus reuelacionum* tradition, they are available in the *Tractatus* version only in Z^a/W^b. As regards the substantial alterations in rev. XI in comparison with *Rev.* VII: 31, obviously made to adapt the revelation to the needs of the new context (see above pp. 28-29), there is no question about which text to edit. But further there are some minor omissions and other alterations. The crucial question is of course: can these differences be attributed to Alfonso's reediting activity (either deliberate modifications, which should be retained in the present edition, or errors found in his copy) or are they later scribal errors of the type we have seen above? These questions are hardly possible to answer and, in order to avoid ending up in a quagmire of arbitrariness, I have decided to follow the manuscript in the main and make a few emendations with reference to the respective chapters in the *Liber celestis*.

3.2. Archetypal errors

In III: 16-17 below, we read an interpretation of a church building in disrepair:

> **16** In uncinis vero, qui postibus coniunguntur, significantur cardinales, qui extenti et effusi sunt, in quantum valent, ad omnem superbiam, cupiditatem et carnis delectamentum. **17** Ideo recipiat papa in manu malleum et forpicem et flectat *cardines* ad velle suum non permittendo eos habere plura de vestibus, de familia et de utensilibus, nisi quantum requirit necessitas et usus vite.

After some of the usual complaints about the moral standard of the cardinals, the pope is asked to bend the *cardines*, the *hinges*, to his will and forbid them to have more clothes, servants and equipment than they absolutely need. A check in the source of this revelation, IV: 49 (in Aili's edition), shows that *cardines* to be sure was the reading of the archetype of the *corpus reuelacionum*, but that two of the eleven manuscripts used for the edition give the reading *cardinales* and one has omitted the word altogether.

Generally speaking, *cardines* can of course be used to signify 'cardinals', but this cannot reasonably be the case here, for in § 16 we learn that *uncini*, hooks, have that function in this revelation (*In uncinis...significantur cardinales*), and in § 10 the *cardines* appear in an alltogether different meaning (*In foraminibus...cardinum significatur humilitas*) and have nothing at all to do with cardinals. In actual fact, even if *cardines* had been used to signify *cardinales* in this revelation, the reading would have been suspicious in § 17, considering the fact that the interpreting is already done in § 16 and § 17 concerns what should be done as a consequence of this interpretation. In the light of this I suggest that *cardines* be emended to *cardinales*, a reading which easily could have been corrupted, since it is often written in abbreviated form in the manuscripts.

In VI: 5 a series of readings is involved:

> [pia mater] filio ... currit, et, ne deficeret (**W**^{b} **yq**; deficiat **KF**) frigore ... eleuauit (**W**^{b} **yq**; eleuat **KF**) eundem, quem ... fouit (**W**^{b} **yq**; fouet **KF**) ... calefecit (**W**^{b} **yq**; calefacit **KF**) ... cibauit (**W**^{b} **yq**; cibat **KF**)

It might be tempting to consider *currit* and the following readings in the present tense to be the authentic readings, for *currit* is undoubtedly in the present tense (the perfect is given as *cucurrit* in the revelations) and requires the present tense in the following verbs as well, but on the other hand the readings of the archetype was in all probability the ones in the past tense. That distribution of readings could be explained if we assume that something was wrong with *currit*. My suggestion is that we read *accurrit*, which can be used in the perfect tense and would make perfect sense in the context (*accurrere* means 'auxilio venire alicui' [*TLL*] or 'to run or hurry to or up to, esp. to help [*OLD*]). Thus, I assume that the first syllable has disappeared, and that *currit* has then given rise to the alteration in **K F** in order to obtain a consistent use of tense, whereas the original readings, which do not square with the present *currit*, have been retained in **W**b **y q**.

3.3. Presentation of the text

Orthography
I have carried out a few normalisations of spelling in accordance with the usage generally observed in the manuscripts.

Apparatus
In the apparatus criticus, I have not listed orthographic divergences or obvious and insignificant miswritings, such as **X R** *reuellatio* and *missit* **W**b, XIII: 6 *monastiche* **K**, XIII: 9 *purgatori* **W**b, or, in the title, *swecie* **K**.

STEMMA CODICUM ADHIBITORUM

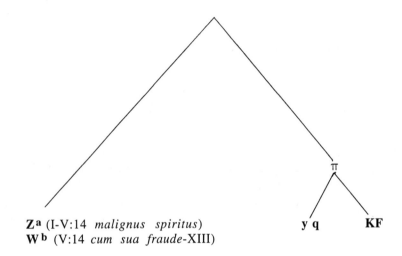

Zᵃ (I-V:14 *malignus spiritus*)
Wᵇ (V:14 *cum sua fraude*-XIII)

y q   **KF**

REUELACIONES INFRASCRIPTAS HABUIT IN VISIONE SPIRITUALI DIUINITUS DEUOTA ANCILLA CHRISTI SANCTE MEMORIE DOMINA BRIGIDA, PRINCIPISSA DE REGNO SUECIE, STANDO IN ORACIONE. QUE DIRIGUNTUR AD SUMMOS PONTIFICES CLEMENTEM VI, INNOCENCIUM VI, URBANUM V, GREGORIUM XI. QUE TRACTANT DE REDUCENDO SEDEM APOSTOLICAM ET ROMANAM CURIAM AD ROMAM ET DE REFORMACIONE ECCLESIE EX PRECEPTO DEI OMNIPOTENTIS.

(I)

Christus per duos annos ante iubileum dat sponse verba hic contenta et precipit illa mittere pape Clementi VI, scilicet quod faceret pacem inter reges Francie et Anglie et quod veniret in Ytaliam et annunciaret annum iubileum, et hanc reuelacionem portauit dominus Hemmingus, episcopus Aboensis et frater Petrus, prior monasterii de Aluastro de regno Suecie ordinis Cisterciensis.

1 Filius Dei loquitur ad sponsam dicens: "Scribe ex parte mea pape Clementi verba hec: Ego exaltaui te et ascendere te feci per omnes gradus honoris. Surge igitur ad faciendum pacem inter reges Francie et Anglie, qui sunt periculose bestie, animarum proditores. **2** Veni deinde in Ytaliam et predica ibi verbum et annum salutis et dileccionis diuine et vide plateas stratas sanctorum meorum sanguine et dabo tibi mercedem illam que non finietur! **3** Attende eciam tempora priora, in qui-

---

For the title, see below p. 63. Cap. I *cf. VI: 63. Alfonso, Informaciones* § *3-11, Conscripcio p. 83-84.* **R** per duos annos ante *sc. 1348. For the meaning of the expression, see Bergh, 'Zeitdifferenzbestimmungen'. On Bishop Hemming's mission, see Klockars, Biskop Hemming, pp. 151-166.* **1** periculose bestie *cf. Rev. IV: 104.*

Titulus operis et rubrica cap. I: **Z**ᵃ yq **KF** § 1-9: **Z**ᵃ y **KF**

BRIGIDA] birgitta **q KF** .b. y   *ex* oracionem *corr.* **Z**ᵃ   PRINCIPISSA *om.* **q K F**
VI] quintum **KF**   XI *bis* **q**   OMNIPOTENTIS *om.* **Z**ᵃ
R dat] dedit **Z**ᵃ   precepit **q**   VI *(vide p. 26)]* quinto **p**   quod² *om.* **Z**ᵃ
de Aluastro *om.* **K** de aluastrom **q** Alvastra **F**   cisterciensis ordinis de regno swecie **KF**   *etc. post* Cisterciensis *add.* **q**   **1** hec verba y
2 in *(vide p. 26)]* ad y **KF**   videas y

bus audacter ad iram prouocasti me et silui, in quibus fecisti que volu-
isti et non debuisti et ego quasi non iudicans paciens fui, **4** quia tempus meum nunc appropinquat et exquiram a te negligenciam et auda-
ciam temporis tui et, sicut per omnes gradus ascendere te feci, sic de-
scendes spiritualiter per alios gradus, quos experieris veraciter in anima et corpore, nisi obedieris verbis meis, **5** et silebit lingua tua magni-
loqua, et nomen tuum, quod vocasti in terris, in obliuione et opprobrio
erit in conspectu meo et sanctorum meorum. Exquiram eciam a te,
quam indigne—permissione tamen mea—ad omnes gradus ascendisti,
quod melius ego Deus scio, quam tua negligens consciencia recordatur.
6 Queram quoque a te, quantum in reformacione pacis regum tepuisti
et quantum in aliam partem declinasti. Insuper non erit in obliuione,
qualiter cupiditas et ambicio in Ecclesia tempore tuo floruit et aucta
est et quod multa reformare et emendare potuisti, sed tu, amator carnis, noluisti. **7** Surge igitur, antequam nouissima hora tua appropin-
quans veniat, et negligencias priorum temporum penultimo tempore
zelando extingue!

Si autem dubitas, cuius spiritus verba ista sint, ecce regnum et
persona nota sunt, in quibus stupor et mirabilia facta sunt. **8** Iusticia
enim et misericordia, de quibus loquor, appropinquant ubique terra-
rum. Consciencia enim tua racionabile dicit esse illud, quod moneo, et
caritatiuum esse, quod suadeo. **9** Et nisi paciencia mea seruasset te,
iam profundius ultra alios predecessores tuos descendisses. Ergo in-
quire in libro consciencie tue et vide, si veritatem loquor!"

---

3 audacter...me *cf. Iob 12, 6 and 4 Reg 23, 26*   silui...paciens fui *cf. Is 42, 14* **5** nomen...terris *cf. Ps. 48, 12* **8** ecce regnum...facta sunt *cf. Prologo magistri Mathie
§ 1 in Undhagen, Rev. I, p. 229.*

---

3 prouocasti me ad iram **F**   iudicans] audiens **KF** **4** descendas **F**
5 quam¹] quod **y**   ego deus melius **KF**   *in* recordatur *corr.* **Z**ᵃ **6** regum *om.* **Z**ᵃ
    floruit tempore tuo **KF** **7** igitur *supra lin.* **F**   et³ *supra lineam* **F**
7-8 et mirabilia...loquor *om.* **y**
8 *ex* tua enim *corr.* **y**   tua *om.* **Z**ᵃ

(II)

Verba Christi ad sponsam mencionem faciencia de papa Innocencio VI, qui fuit post Clementem.

1 Filius loquitur ad sponsam dicens: "Iste papa Innocencius est de ere meliori quam antecessor eius et materia apta ad suscipiendum colores optimos, sed malicia hominum exigit, ut cicius tollatur de medio. **2** Cui voluntas sua bona reputabitur in coronam et glorie augmentacionem. Verumptamen, si verba mea librorum tibi data audiret, fieret melior, et qui deferrent ad eum verba, sublimius coronarentur."

(III)

Una die antequam papa Urbanus V intraret Romam, habuit domina Brigida infrascriptam reuelacionem in Sancta Maria Maiori in Roma, que tractat de reparacione Ecclesie.

1 Uni persone videbatur, quasi quod esset in magno choro, et apparuit sol magnus et lucens, dueque sedes quasi predicatorum in choro erant, una a dextris aliaque a sinistris distantes a sole longo spacio et interuallo, duoque radii de sole ad sedes procedebant.

2 Tunc vox audiebatur de sede, que ad sinistram partem erat, dicens: "Aue, rex in eternum creator et redemptor iustusque iudex, ecce vicarius tuus, qui sedet in sede tua in mundo, reduxit iam sedem in

---

Cap. II *cf. IV 136.* **1** malicia hominum *Gn 6, 5*

Cap. III *cf. IV: 49*   **R** Una die antequam *sc. October 15, 1367.*

Cap. II: **Z ª yq KF**
1 dicens *om.* **K** *supra lin.* **F**   suscipiendum] suscipiendos **Z ª** recipiendum **KF** *in suscipiendos ut videtur alt.* **q**
2 defferent **Z ª** different **y**   verba *om.* **q**

Rubrica cap. III: **Z ª yq** *infra columnam add.* **K** 2   **§ 1-21: Z ª**
R Papa *om.* **K**   V *om.* **y**   domina] beata **K**   Brigida] Birgitta **q K B y**   S a n c t a
Maria Maiori]   in ecclesia sancte marie maiori **K**   **1** a 2 ad **Z ª**

antiquum et priorem locum, ubi sedit primus papa Petrus, qui fuit princeps apostolorum."

3 Respondit vox de dextra sede dicens: "Quomodo," inquit, "poterit intrare in sanctam Ecclesiam, in qua foramina cardinum sunt plena rubigine et terra? **4** Ideo et postes inclinati sunt ad terram, quia in foraminibus non est locus, ubi uncini imprimantur, qui postes debent sustentare. Uncini quoque sunt extenti ad plenum nichilque curuati ad postes tenendum. **5** Pauimentum vero totum effossum est et conuersum in foueas profundas ad modum puteorum profundissimorum, qui nullum omnino habent fundum. **6** Tectum autem est linitum pice et ardet de igne sulfureo stillans quasi pluuia densa. **7** De nigredine vero et spissitudine fumi, qui de abisso fossarum et de stillicidiis tecti ascendit, omnes parietes maculati sunt et ita deformes in colore ad intuendum quasi sanguis commixtus putrida sanie. **8** Ideo amiculum Dei non decet mansionem habere in tali templo."

9 Respondit vox de sede ad partem sinistram: "Expone," inquit, "spiritualiter que dixisti corporaliter." **10** Tunc ait vox: "Papa similatur et designatur in postibus. In foraminibus vero cardinum significatur humilitas, que sic vacua debet esse ab omni superbia, ut nichil appareat in ea, nisi quod pertinet ad officium humile pontificale, sicut foramen debet esse vacuum totaliter a rubigine. **11** Sed iam foramina, id est humilitatis insignia sunt ita repleta superfluitatibus et diuiciis et facultatibus, que ad nichil aliud custodiuntur et possidentur nisi ad superbiam, quod nichil apparet humile, quia tota humilitas conuersa est ad mundanam pompam. **12** Ideo non mirum, quod papa, qui similatur in postibus, inclinatus est ad mundialia, que significantur in rubigine et in terra. **13** Propterea papa incipiat veram humilitatem in se ipso, primo in apparatu suo, in vestibus, in auro et argento et vasis argenteis, in equis et aliis utensilibus, segregando de eis omnibus sola necessaria sua, alia vero erogando pauperibus et specialiter hiis, quos nouerit amicos Dei. **14** Deinde moderate disponat familiam suam et necessarios habeat famulos, qui vitam suam custodiant, **15** quia licet in manu Dei est, quando {ei} velit vocare eum ad iudicium, iustum tamen est quod habeat famulos propter roborandam iusticiam et ut

---

8 decet *scripsi rev. IV: 49 secutus* debet **Z**ᵃ   *ex* habere mansionem *alt.* **Z**ᵃ
12 est *supra lin. add* **Z**ᵃ   in *del.* **Z**ᵃ   15 eum *supra lin. add* **Z**ᵃ

eos, qui se contra Deum et sancte Ecclesie consuetudinem erigunt, valeat humiliare.

16 In uncinis vero, qui postibus coniunguntur, significantur cardinales, qui extenti et effusi sunt, in quantum valent, ad omnem superbiam et cupiditatem et carnis delectamentum. **17** Ideo recipiat papa in manu malleum et forpicem et flectat cardin<al>es ad velle suum non permittendo eos habere plura de vestibus, de familia et de utensilibus, nisi quantum requirit necessitas et usus vite, **18** flectatque eos forpice, id est verbis lenibus et consilio diuino paternaque caritate. Qui si noluerint obedire, recipiat malleum scilicet ostendendo eis seueritatem suam faciendoque quicquid poterit, quod tamen non sit contra iusticiam, donec flectantur ad velle suum.

19 In pauimento autem significantur episcopi et clerici seculares, quorum cupiditas nullum habet fundum. De quorum superbia et vita luxuriosa procedit fumus, ob quem abhominantur omnes angeli in celis et amici Dei in terris. **20** Ista enim emendare potest papa in multis, si unumquemque permittat habere necessaria non superflua precipiatque unicuique episcopo attendere ad cleri sui vitam. **21** Et quicumque noluerit emendare vitam suam et stare in continencia, priuetur omnino prebenda sua, quia carius est Deo, quod in illo loco non dicatur missa, quam quod manus meretricee tangant corpus Dei."

---

17 cardinales *scripsi, vide p. 36* cardines **Z**[a]   **18** *in* eis *corr.* **Z**[a]   **20** permittat *ex* permittit *alt.* **Z**[a]

Reuelacio tangens papam Urbanum, quam habuit sponsa Christi in Roma super confirmacione regule Saluatoris et super indulgenciis Sancti Petri ad vincula a Christo concessis monasterio beate Brigide.

1 Filius Dei loquitur ad sponsam: "Qui habet glomeracionem filorum, in qua est intus aurum optimum, non desinit filare, donec inuenerit aurum. Quo inuento utitur eo possessor ad honorem et commodum suum. **2** Sic iste papa Urbanus aurum est ductile ad bona sed sollicitudinibus mundi vallatus est. **3** Ideo vade et dic ei ex parte mea: 'Tempus tuum breue est. Surge et attende, quomodo anime tibi commisse saluentur! Ego optuli tibi regulam religionis, que fundari et incipi debet in loco Watzstenom in Suecia, que de ore meo processit. **4** Nunc autem volo, ut non solum auctoritate tua confirmetur sed et benediccione tua, qui vicarius meus es in terris, roboretur. **5** Ego dictaui eam et dotaui spirituali dote, scilicet concedendo indulgencias, que sunt in ecclesia Sancti Petri ad vincula in Roma. Tu ergo approba coram hominibus quod coram exercitu meo celesti est sanctitum!' **6** Si autem queris signum, quod hec ego loquor, hoc iam ostendi tibi, quia quando primum audisti verba mea, anima tua in aduentu nuncii mei spiritualiter fuit consolata. Si autem queris ulterius signum, dabitur tibi, sed non sicut Ione prophete. **7** Tu autem, sponsa mea, cui dictam graciam feci, si non poteris habere litteram et graciam pape et sigillum super concessione dicte indulgencie nisi precedente pecunia, sufficit tibi benediccio mea. **8** Ego enim approbabo et confirmabo verbum meum, et omnes sancti erunt tibi testes, mater mea sit tibi sigillum,

---

Cap. IV *cf. IV: 137 and Reu. ex. 44* **5** *On the so-called Regula in prima persona, see Eklund, Regula, pp. 21-23* **6** queris signum *cf Ex 4, 1-9; below X: 2-5.*

Cap. IV: Z^a **yq KF**
R sancti *ante* Saluatoris *add.* **F** Brigide] b **y** birgitte **q** virginis in watzsteno **K F** **1** glomationem Z^a intus *om.* **K** *supra lin.* **F** defilare Z^a utitur *om.* Z^a **3** Tempus tuum breue est *om.* **q** est *om.* **y** regulam *in marg. add.* K^2 loco] castro Z^a uazteni Z^a wazsten **y** watzsteno **q** **4** et] etiam quod Z^a eciam **q** in terris es **yq K** et *post* es *add.* **y** **5** ad vincula sancti petri Z^a ergo] igitur **y** ergo approba] approba ergo eam Z^a sancsitum Z^a **6** aduentum Z^a sed *om.* **K** *supra lin.* **F** **7** graciam et litteram Z^a indulgencie dicte **KF** **8** tibi[1] michi **K** *in* tibi *corr.* **F**

pater meus confirmator et Spiritus Sanctus adueniencium ad tuum monasterium consolator."

(V)

Hec est reuelacio, quam habuit sponsa Christi in Roma de eodem papa Urbano, antequam rediret Auinionem anno Domini MCCCLXX, quam ipsa presentauit ei in monte Flasconis.

1 Vigilante de nocte prefata persona, in oracione visum fuit sibi, ac si una vox loqueretur procedens a quodam circulo splendoris ad modum solis. Que quidem vox dixit sibi hec verba, que sequuntur:

2 "Ego sum mater Dei, quia sic placuit sibi. Ego eciam sum mater omnium, qui sunt in superno gaudio. Quamuis infantes habeant suam necessitatem secundum suam voluntatem, tamen in augmentum sue leticie cumulatur eis gaudium ex eo, quod vident faciem matris sue blandam. **3** Sic placet Deo dare omnibus in celesti curia gaudium et exultacionem de mee virginitatis puritate et mearum virtutum pulcritudine, quamuis habeant incomprehensibiliter ex eius diuinitatis potencia totum bonum. **4** Sum eciam mater omnium, qui sunt in purgatorio, quia omnes pene, que debentur purgandis pro peccatis suis, in qualibet hora propter preces meas quodammodo mitigantur. Ita placet Deo, et alique ex hiis penis, que debentur eis de rigore diuine iusticie, minuuntur. **5** Ego sum eciam mater tocius iusticie, que est in mundo, quam iusticiam filius meus dilexit dileccione perfectissima. Et sicut

Cap. V *cf. IV: 138. Presented to the pope on 14 August in the presence of Alfonso and Cardinal Beaufort (later Pope Gregory XI), who was the only cardinal who learnt about this terrible message (Alfonso, Informaciones § 20-29, Conscripcio pp. 85-86); Jönsson, Alfonso, p. 43-47*

monasterium tuum **K F**

V: **Z**ᵃ (**1-14** malignus spiritus) **W**ᵇ (**14** cum sua fraude-**18**) *vide n. 18* **yq KF**

R ad *ante* Auinionem *add.* **Z**ᵃ   Domini *om.* y *ex* ccc lxx *alt.* **Z**ᵃ **1** dixit sibi *bis* y **2** sibi] ei **Z**ᵃ   suam necessitatem *om.* K gaudium **F** *(vide p. 00)*   gaudium *ante* faciem *del.* y   **3** pulcritudinem y   **4** ex] de **K**   **5** meus *ante* filius *del.* **F** dilectione dilexit **Z**ᵃ

matera manus parata est ad opponendum se periculis in cordis filii
sui defensionem, si aliquis niteretur in sui lesione, ita ego sum parata
iugiter iustos, qui sunt in mundo, defendere et de omni spirituali periculo liberare. **6** Ego eciam sum quasi mater omnium peccatorum se
volencium emendare et habencium voluntatem in Deum amplius non
peccare et sum voluntaria ipsum peccatorem in meam defensionem
accipere sicut caritatiua mater, dum viderit filium suum nudum ab inimicis acutos gladios habentibus sibi occurrentem. **7** Nonne ipsa tunc
opponeret se periculis viriliter, ut filium suum de manibus inimicorum
suorum liberaret et eriperet et in sinu suo gaudenter conseruaret? **8**
Ita facio et faciam ego omnibus peccatoribus misericordiam a filio meo
petentibus sub vera contricione et diuina dileccione.

9 Audi tu et attende diligenter, quid ego volo dicere de duobus fili-
is meis, quos tibi volo nominare. Primus, quem dico, est filius meus
Iesus Christus, qui natus est de mea carne virginea ad hoc, ut suam
caritatem manifestaret et animas redimeret, **10** propter quod non pe-
percit sui corporis laboribus nec sui sanguinis effusionibus nec dedig-
natus est audire contumelias et sustinere sue mortis penam. Ille est
ipse Deus et est omnipotens in eterna leticia. **11** Secundus, quem re-
puto pro filio meo, est ille, qui residet in papali sede, in sede Dei in
mundo, si obedierit preceptis suis et ipsum dilexerit perfecta caritate.

12 Modo volo aliquid loqui super isto papa, qui nominatur Urbanus. Propter precem meam obtinuit ipse Spiritus Sancti infusionem, ut
deberet ad Romam et Ytaliam declinare ad nichil aliud, nisi ut misericordiam et iusticiam faceret, fidem catholicam roboraret, pacem refor-
maret et sic sanctam Ecclesiam innouaret. **13** Sicut mater ducit filium
suum ad locum, ubi sibi placet, dum ostendit sibi ubera sua, ita duxi
ego Urbanum papam mea prece et opere Spiritus Sancti de Auinione
ad Romam sine quouis suo periculo corporali. **14** Quid fecerat ipse
michi? Iam vertit ad me dorsum et non faciem et intendit a me rece-
dere, et ducit eum ad hoc malignus spiritus cum sua fraude, nam
tedium habet de diuino labore et libitum ad suum commodum corpo-

---

semper *ante* parata *add.* **K F**   periculo **KF**   lesionem **KF**   **6** se *ante* emendare *del.* **F**   voluntariam **Z ᵃ**   accipere] recipere **y**   caritiua **q**   videt **K F**
suis *post* inimicis *add.* **q**   accurrente **Z ᵃ**   **9** primum **y**   caritatem suam **F**
10 mortis] corporis **y**   penas **Z ᵃ**   **11** ille est **Z ᵃ**   **12** aliquid *om.* **F**   isto] ipso **Z ᵃ**
        ad *ante* Ytaliam *add.* **K**   **13** sua *om.* **Z ᵃ**   ego duxi **F**   opere] ope **F**
periculo suo **K F**

rale. **15** Item trahit eum dyabolus cum delectacione mundiali, nam nimis desiderio est sibi terra nacionis sue mundano more. Item trahitur carnalium amicorum consiliis, qui magis attendunt suam delectacionem et voluptatem quam Dei honorem et voluntatem vel anime sue profectum et salutem. **16** Si contigerit ipsum redire ad terras, ubi fuit electus papa, ipse habebit in breui tempore unam percussionem siue alapam, quod dentes sui stringent seu strident, visus caligabit et fuscus erit et tocius sui corporis membra contremiscent, **17** ardor Spiritus Sancti paulisper tepescet in eo et recedet et omnium amicorum Dei preces, qui pro ipso orare decreuerunt lacrimis gemebundis, torpebunt et corda ad eius dileccionem frigescent, **18** et de duobus coram Deo reddet racionem: primo de hiis que fecerat in papali sede, secundo de hiis que omiserat ex hiis, que potuisset in Dei honore fecisse in sua magna maiestate."

(VI)

Hec que sequitur est reuelacio prima que fuit missa domino Gregorio pape XI per dominum Latinum de Ursinis.

1 Una persona vigilans et non dormiens sed in oracione persistens in spiritu rapta fuit, et tunc omnes eius corporis vires quasi deficere videbantur, sed cor ipsius inflammabatur et exultabat caritatis ardore eiusque anima consolabatur, et quodam diuino robore confortabatur spiritus eius, ac eciam tota consciencia eius replebatur intellectu spirituali. **2** Cui persone tunc apparuit visio talis. Audiebat enim ipsa tunc

---

Cap. VI *cf. IV: 139. Alfonso, Epistola Solitarii IV: 12-13, Informaciones §§ 30-33, Conscripcio, p. 86.*

---

15 delectacionem] dileccionem **q**   voluptatem (*cf. Bergh, Rev. VI, p. 44)*] voluntatem **π**   **16** contingerit **W** contingeret **q**   stringent] stringente **y**   stridebunt **F**   **17** recedit **q**   ipso] eo **F**   cor *in* corda *corr.* **y**   **18** de hiis *om.* **W** [b]   honorem **W** [b]   maiestate] potestate **q**

VI: **W** [b] **yq KF**
R sequuntur **W** [b]   est *supra lin.* **F**   domina **y**   de *om.* **q**   **1** tunc omnes eius]
omnes tunc **W** [b]   corporis eius **KF**   eius consciencia **F**   **2** ipsa] illa **F**

47

quandam vocem dulcisonam eam taliter alloquentem: "Ego sum illa que genui Dei filium, verum Deum, Iesum Christum. **3** Quoniam alias dixi tibi aliqua verba, que Urbano pape deberent nunciari, nunc eciam dico tibi aliqua, que mittenda sunt pape Gregorio. Sed ut melius intelligantur, dicam tibi ea per quandam similitudinem. **4** Sicut enim pia mater dilectum videns filium suum nudum et frigidum in terra iacentem et ad erigendum se vires corporis nullas habentem, sed pre desiderio fauoris et lactis materni querulis vocibus cum vagitu plorantem, **5** que tunc tenera dileccione compassa filio festine accurrit et, ne deficeret frigore, pia manu materna de terra eleuauit eundem, quem statim leniter fouit et materno calore sui pectoris mitissime calefecit eumque dulciter mamillarum suarum lacte cibauit, **6** sic ego mater misericordie facere volo pape Gregorio, si in Romam et Ytaliam redire voluerit animo permanendi et voluntatem habuerit ibidem, ut pius pastor, plangendi compassionis lacrimis gemebundis animarum sibi ouium commissarum eternam perdicionem et earum dampna et dispendia dolorosa et innouare proposuerit statum Ecclesie cum humilitate et pastorali debita caritate.

7 Tunc enim ego sicut pia mater eleuabo eum de terra velut nudum filium frigidum, id est separabo eum et totum eius cor ab omni delectacione terrena et ab omni mundano amore, que sunt contra Dei voluntatem, et calefaciam eum suauiter materno calore scilicet caritatis mee, que est in pectore meo. **8** Saturabo eciam eum lacte meo, id est oracione mea, que similis est lacti. O, quam innumerabiles sunt illi, qui lacte oracionis mee sustentantur et dulciter saturantur! **9** Isto enim lacte saturabo eum, id est oracione mea, quam faciam pro eo ad Dominum et Deum meum, qui est filius meus, ut ipse dignetur miscere et unire spiritum suum sanctum cum interno sanguine cordis eiusdem Gregorii pape. **10** Tunc autem ipse saciabitur vera societate perfecte in

---

deum verum **W** [b]   **3** tibi dico **W** [b]   intelligas **K**   dicam ea tibi **F**
quandam] aliquam **F**   **4** videns dilectum **W** [b]   pre] pro **KF**
5 accurrit *scripsi (cf. p. 36-37)* currit **W** [b] π   deficiat **KF**   materna manu **y**
eleuat **KF** leuauit **W** [b]   ipsum **KF**   quem] Que **W** [b]   fouet **KF**   materno *ex*
mater *corr.* **W** [b]   calefacit **KF**   cibat **KF**   **6** in *ante* Ytaliam *add.* **F**
ibidem *om.* **F**   ouium *(cf. IX: 9-10)*] omnium **W**[b] **F**   **7** ego *om.* **KF**   cor eius **W** [b]
sunt] sint **W** [b]   voluntatem dei **W** [b]   **8** eum] ipsum **q KF**
9 miscere] misereri **y**

tantum, quod ulterius ad nichil aliud desiderabit in hoc seculo viuere, nisi ut possit Dei honorem totis suis viribus augmentare. **11** Ecce iam nunc ostendi ei maternam caritatem, quam sibi faciam, si obedierit, quia voluntas Dei est, ut transferat sedem suam ad Romam cum humilitate. **12** Modo eciam, ne in posterum ipse ignorancia excusetur, ego precauens eum caritate materna annuncio ei ista, que sequuntur, videlicet quod si predictis ipse non obedierit, indubitanter senciet iusticie virgam, id est filii mei indignacionem, quia tunc abbreuiabitur vita eius et vocabitur ad iudicium Dei. **13** Nulla tunc ei temporalium potestas auxiliabitur dominorum, non eciam sapiencia et sciencia ei proderunt medicorum nec flatus aeris sue natalis patrie proficiet ei ad eius vitam aliquatenus prorogandam."

---

10 quod] ut **Y**   totis] totius **W** b   **11** faciam sibi **y KF**   ut] quod **W** b
12 ipse ignorantia imposterum **W** b   ipse¹ *om.* **KF**   ego] eum **y**
13 eciam] ei **y KF**   ei *ante* proderunt *om.* **KF**   natalis] naturalis **q** natalis *ex fortasse* naturalis *corr.* **F**   prorogandam] prolongandam **W** b
Post prorogandam *addunt* π (**q** *autem om. § 16*): **14** Quasi dicat, quod si eciam venerit romam et predicta non fecerit, tunc abbreuiabitur eius vita (vita eius **q**) nec proderunt ei medici nec reuertetur ad auinionem, vbi possit ei proficere aer natalis patrie sed pocius morietur. **15** Nota ista quatuor sequencia, que precipiuntur pape, scilicet quod veniat romam cum humilitate, secundo quod animo permanendi, tercio quod plangat (*ex* plangat quod *corr.* **y**) dampna perdicionum animarum, quarto quod renouare conetur (tenetur **q**) ecclesiam dei (dei *om.* **yq**) etc, **16** que omnia si non fecerit, abbreuiabitur eius vita (vita eius **y**), ut habetur superius ibi "modo eciam" (superius ibi "modo eciam"] id est capitulo ci **y**) etc (etc *om.* **K**). Et ideo non sufficit pape quod solummodo veniat romam, nisi perficiet (-at **y**) illa supradicta quatuor, que ei precipiuntur.
Post precipiuntur *addunt* **y K**: pro hoc facit cardinalis (?) quod (quod *om.* **K**) habetur infra (infra *om.* **K**) in reuelacione que incipit pater sancte etc (etc *om.* **K**) veni igitur cum sequentibus [IX:13].

VII

Sequitur alia visio, quam portauit dominus comes de Nola eidem pape Gregorio XI.

1 Laus sit Deo pro omni dileccione sua et seruicium et honor sanctissime Marie, preciose virgini, sue matri pro compassione, quam habet super omnes, quos filius suus redemit suo sanguine precioso! **2** Pater sancte, hinc est quod cuidam persone, quam vos bene nostis vigilando in oracione existenti contigit, quod senciebat cor suum totum inflammari diuine caritatis ardore et quadam visitacione Spiritus Sancti. **3** Que quidem persona tunc audiuit quandam vocem sibi dicentem: "Audi tu, que vides spiritualia et dicito illud, quod tibi modo precipitur, et scribe Gregorio summo pontifici hec verba, que modo audies. **4** Ego, que modo loquor tibi, sum illa, quam Deo placuit sibi in matrem eligere, qui de carne mea sibi assumpsit corpus humanum. Ipse quidem filius meus fecit cum Gregorio papa magnum opus misericordie, quando scilicet per me fecit sibi dici sanctissimam suam voluntatem, quam in priori reuelacione sibi transmissa ei plenius intimaui, **5** et hoc factum est pocius propter oraciones et lacrimas amicorum Dei quam propter eius aliqua merita precedencia. Ideo ego et dyabolus, inimicus eius, grande certamen habuimus super eum, **6** nam ego monui eundem Gregorium papam in alia littera, ut festinanter ad Romam seu Ytaliam se transferret cum humilitate et diuina caritate et ut ibidem suam sedem poneret et usque ad mortem omnino permaneret. **7** Dyabolus vero et alii consiliarii eiusdem pape consuluerunt ei tardare et in illis, ubi nunc est, partibus demorari et hoc propter carnalem amorem et eciam propter parentum et amicorum carnalium mundanam delectacionem et consolacionem. **8** Et ideo dyabolus maiorem nunc habet ius-

---

Cap. VII *cf. IV: 140. Alfonso, Informaciones §§ 34-36, Conscripcio p. 86.*

VII: **W**[b] **yq KF**
R alia visio] alia visio secunda **W**[b] **q** visio secunda **KF**   portauit *om.* y
1 deo sit **y KF**   virginis **W**[b]   redemerit **q**   **2** quadam] qua y   **3** audis y
4 sibi *ante* eligere *tpt.* **KF**   sumpsit y **KF**   fecit[1] facit **q**   suam sanctissimam **W**[b]   ei *om.* **q**   **6** transferet **W**[b]   omnimode **W**[b]   **7** alii] aliqui **y q**
et[4] ac **W**[b]

ticiam et occasionem temptandi eum, quia magis obediuit consilio dyaboli et amicorum carnalium quam Dei et mee uoluntati.

9 Verum quia ipse papa desiderat de uoluntate Dei adhuc plenius certificari, ideo iustum est, ut tale suum desiderium impleatur. Nouerit ergo certissime hoc, quod infra sequitur, esse uoluntatis Dei, **10** videlicet quod sine dilacione quacumque ipse veniat ad Ytaliam seu Romam et omnino taliter faciat et acceleret iter suum cum festinancia ad veniendum, quod in mense Marcii vel ad ultimum in toto Aprili proxime futuro ipse personaliter in predicta urbe seu prouincia Ytalie omnino sit ingressus, si ipse umquam in matrem voluerit me habere. **11** Si autem in predictis inobediens fuerit, veraciter sciat, quod numquam amplius tali consolacione, id est alia mea visitacione seu reuelacione visitabitur in hoc mundo sed post mortem suam respondebit coram diuina iusticia, cur mandatis meis noluerit obedire. **12** Si vero in predictis obedierit, tunc eciam ego complebo ea, que promisi in reuelacione illa a me sibi primitus destinata.

13 Notum eciam facio eidem pape, quod numquam erit sic firma et tranquilla pax in Francia, quod habitantes in ea plena securitate et concordia possint ullatenus congaudere, antequam populus illius regni placauerit Deum filium meum per aliqua magna opera pietatis et humilitatis, quem suis multis peccatis et offensionibus ad indignacionem et iram hactenus prouocauerunt.

14 Propterea nouerit, quod iter seu passagium illorum armigerorum de iniquis societatibus iniquorum, quod ipsi facere volunt ad sanctum sepulcrum filii mei, non magis placet eidem filio meo vero Deo quam aurum illud, quod populus Israel proiecit in ignem, de quo dyabolus conflatilem vitulum compaginauit, quia in eis est superbia et cupiditas. **15** Et si aliquam habent voluntatem eundi ad memoratum

---

9-12, 13, 14-15 *This revelation was received in answer to three questions asked by the pope, see Alfonso, Conscripcio p. 86.*

---

9 adimpleatur y   ergo] igitur q *supra lin.* F² *om.* y K   **10** vel *om.* K *in marg. add.* F²   in toto] intrante KF   Ytalia y KF   omnino] omnimode W ᵇ   me voluerit W ᵇ   **11** respondit F   meis] dei KF   **12** ego eciam W ᵇ   illa *om.* q   a me *post* primitus *tpt.* y   *ex* destinatas *corr.* q   **13** possunt K F   populi W ᵇ q   placauerint q KF   peccatis *(cf. pp. 26-27)*] penis yq prauis operibus KF   **14** meo *om.* W ᵇ

sepulcrum, magis est propter superbiam et cupiditatem pecunie quam propter amorem et honorem Dei." Et hiis dictis hec visio disparuit.

16 Post hec autem subiunxit et dixit michi mater Dei: "Item dic episcopo meo heremite, quod claudat istam litteram et sigillet eam et postea scribat in alia papiro copiam eius et ostendat eandem copiam apertam illi abbati nuncio pape et Nolano comiti, ut ipsi legant illam et sciant, quid continetur in ea. 17 Postquam vero ipsi eam legerint, dimittat eis supradictam litteram clausam, sigillatam, quam ipsi statim mittant pape Gregorio sine mora. Sed copiam illam apertam postquam legerint, non dimittat eis, sed volo, quod dilaceret et rumpat eam coram oculis eorum in frusta. 18 Quia sicut littera illa, que est una, dilacerabitur in multa frusticula, sic, nisi papa tempore et anno prefixo venerit in Ytaliam, terre Ecclesie, que sub una eius obediencia et subieccione modo eidem obediunt, diuidentur in plures partes in manus tyrannorum. 19 Et firmissime scias, quod in augmentum tribulacionis ipsius pape non solum ipse audiet sed et videbit oculis suis esse vera que dico, nec poterit cum tota manu potencie sue reducere terras predictas Ecclesie ad pristinum statum sue obediencie et pacis. 20 Ista enim verba, que nunc tibi dico, adhuc non sunt dicenda nec scribenda illi abbati, quia semen occultatur in terra, donec fructificet in spicam."

16-18 *see below p. 68-69.*

15 Et hiis...disparuit *om.* **W** **b**   visio hec **F**   16 istam] illam **y**   alia] alio **W** **b** **y**
17 eam[1] *om.* **F**   legerint eam **q**   clausam *om.* **W** **b**   dimittat[2] dimittet **y**   frusta]
frustra **W** **b**   18 illa littera *ex* illa que littera *alt.* **y**   illa *om.* **K F**   19 esse] ea **y**
Ecclesie *supra lin.* **K**   sue statum **W** **b**   20 enim] autem **W** **b**   dico tibi **y KF**

VIII

Reuelacio quam habuit domina Brigida in Neapoli in festo Sancti Poli-
carpi, quando rediit de Ierusalem, sed hanc reuelacionem non misit
pape, quia non fuit ei preceptum diuinitus.

1 Christus apparuit domine Brigide oranti pro papa Gregorio XI et dixit
ei: "Attende, filia, ad verba que loquor! Scias enim, quod iste papa
Gregorius est similis paralitico, qui non mouet manus ad operandum
nec pedes ad ambulandum. **2** Sicut enim infirmitas paralisis generatur
ex sanguine et humore corrupto et frigore, sic istum papam tenet quasi
ligatum et impeditum immoderatus amor sanguinis sui et frigus
tepiditatis mentis sue ad me. **3** Sed scias, quod adiutorio oracionis
virginis matris mee iam ipse incipiet mouere manus et pedes, scilicet
faciendo voluntatem meam et honorem meum in veniendo Romam.
Ideo scias certissime, quod ipse veniet Romam et ibi inchoabit viam ad
aliqua bona futura, sed non consumabit."

    4 Tunc autem respondit domina Brigida: "O, domine Deus meus,
regina Neapolis et multi alii dicunt michi, quod impossibile est eum
venire Romam, quia rex Francie et cardinales et alii quamplurima ei
ponunt impedimenta ad veniendum. **5** Et audiui, quod multi insurgunt
ibi dicentes se habere spiritum Dei et diuinas reuelaciones et visiones,
qui pretextu illarum dissuadent ei venire, et ideo timeo multum, quod
impediatur aduentus eius."

    6 Respondit dominus: "Audisti legi, quod Ieremias erat in diebus
illis in Israel. Qui habebat spiritum Dei ad prophetandum, et multi
erant tunc, qui habebant spiritum sompniorum et mendacii, quibus rex

---

Cap. VIII *cf. IV: 141.* **R** in festo Sancti Policarpi *sc. February 23rd.*

VIII: **W** **b** **yq KF**
R Reuelacio quam habuit domina Brigida in Neapoli in festo Sancti Policarpi **W** **b**]
Hec facta (facta *om.* **q**) fuit reuelacio in Neapoli predicte sponse Christi pro
eodem (pro eodem *om.* **q**) in festo sancti policarpi **yq** Reuelacio facta sponse in
Neapoli pro eodem **KF**   **1** domine] beate **F**   Brigide] birgitte **q F B K y**
ad verba *om.* **W** **b**   ad³ *om.* **q**   **2** corrupto *post* frigore *add.* **W** **b**   sic] sed **y**
ligatum *om.* **q** ligatum et *om.* **y KF**   frigus] frigor **KF**   **3** oracionis *om.* **y F**
     marie *post* virginis *add.* **KF**   **4** domina *om.* **W** **b** beata **F**   Brigida]
birgitta **yq F B K**   neapoli **W** **b**   ponunt] imponunt **W** **b**   **5** ibi] sibi **W** **b**
reuelaciones et *om.* **W** **b**   qui] que **y**   **6** spiritum *om.* **W** **b**

iniquus credidit, et ideo venit ipse rex in captiuitatem et populus cum eo, nam si rex credidisset soli Ieremie, ablata fuisset ira mea ab eo. **7** Sic eciam et nunc est, quia siue surgant sapientes siue surgant sompniatores siue surgant amici non spiritus sed carnis ipsius Gregorii pape et suadeant et dissuadeant contrarium. Nichilominus tamen ego Dominus preualebo eis et ducam ipsum papam ad Romam non ad eorum consolacionem. **8** Sed utrum tu videbis eum venire vel non, tibi non est hoc licitum scire."

(IX)

Hec fuit reuelacio in Neapoli predicte sponse Christi in mense Februarii pro eodem papa Gregorio anno domini MCCCLXXIII. Quam portauit ei quidam heremita, qui episcopatum renunciauerat.

1 Pater sancte, illa persona, quam bene nouit sanctitas vestra, existens in oracione vigilans, cum staret tunc in raptu mentis contemplacione suspensa, vidit in spiritu similitudinem throni, in quo sedebat similitudo hominis, inestimabilis pulcritudinis et incomprehensibilis potencie dominus, **2** et in circuitu throni stabat multitudo magna sanctorum et innumerabilis exercitus angelorum, et ante sedentem in throno stabat remote quidam episcopus indutus pontificalibus ornamentis.

3 Ipse autem dominus, qui in throno sedebat, michi loquebatur sic dicens: "Michi data est omnis potestas in celo et in terra a patre meo. Et licet tibi videor loqui quasi de uno ore, attamen non solus loquor, quia Pater loquitur mecum et Spiritus Sanctus, que tres persone unum sumus in diuinitatis substancia."

Cap. IX *cf. IV: 142. Alfonso, Informaciones §§ 39-46, Conscripcio p. 87.*

----

7 et[1] *om.* **K F**   quia *om.* **y**   surgant[1] surgunt **q**   sompniaciones *ut videtur* **q** surgant[3] surgunt **q**   pape gregorii **y q**   ad[1] *om.* **W** [b]   **8** vel] an **y**

IX: W [b] **y q K F**
R Hec...MCCCLXXIII **y q**] Hec fuerunt reuelata neapoli pr. sp. chr. in m. feb. pro eod. pap. greg. A. d. ccc°lxxiii° m° **W** [b] Reuelacio facta sponse in neapoli de eodem papa gregorio **K F**   **1** in raptu] rapta **y**   **2** sedentem] sedem **y**
3 videor tibi **K F** *in* tibi videor *alt.* **q**   solus non **W** [b]   que] qui **y q**
sumus unum **q**

4 Deinde ad illum episcopum loquebatur dicens: "Audi, Gregori papa undecime, verba, que ego loquor tecum, et diligenter attende ad ea que tibi dico! **5** Cur tantum odis me aut quare tanta est audacia tua et presumpcio tua contra me? Nam curia tua mundana depredatur celestem curiam meam. Tu vero superbe spolias me ouibus meis. Bona quoque ecclesiastica, que mea propria sunt, et bona subditorum Ecclesie mee tu indebite extorques et surripis, et das illa amicis tuis temporalibus. **6** Tu eciam bona rapis et recipis iniustc a pauperibus meis, et illa das et distribuis indecenter diuitibus tuis, propter quod nimia est audacia et presumpcio tua, eo quod tu tam temere intras curiam meam et non parcis eis, que mea propria sunt. **7** Quid feci tibi, Gregori? Ego quidem pacienter permisi te ascendere ad summum pontificatum et predixi tibi voluntatem meam per litteras de Roma tibi diuina reuelacione transmissas, ammonendo te per illas de salute anime tue, et precautaui te in eis de magno dispendio tuo. **8** Quid igitur pro tantis beneficiis rependis michi? Et quid facis hoc, videlicet quod in curia tua regnat superbia maxima, cupiditas insaciabilis et luxuria michi execrabilis ac eciam vorago pessima horribilis symonie? **9** Insuper et tu eciam rapis et depredaris a me innumerabiles animas, nam quasi omnes, qui veniunt ad curiam tuam, mittis in Gehennam ignis ex eo, quod non diligenter attendis ea que pertinent ad curiam meam, quia tu es preatus et pastor mearum ouium, **10** et ideo culpa tua est, quod non discrete consideras ea que ad spiritualem salutem ipsarum facienda et corrigenda sunt.

11 Et quamuis ex predictis possem secundum iusticiam licite condempnare te, tamen ex misericordia adhuc iterum moneo te de salute anime tue, videlicet ut venias Romam ad sedem tuam, quam cicius poteris. Tempus enim pono in arbitrio tuo. **12** Scias tamen, quod quanto plus tardaueris, tanto plus diminuuntur profectus anime tue et omnium tuarum virtutum, et quanto cicius ad Romam veneris, tanto cicius accrescent tibi virtutes et dona Spiritus Sancti et inflammaberis

---

4 ego *om.* **y**   **5** aut *om.* **KF**   tanta] tantum **F**   tua[1] *om.* **y**   curiam meam celestem **KF**   *ex* me spolias *alt.* **y**   **6** tua *post* audacia *tpt.* **KF**   **7** tibi feci **q** feci] fecit **W**[b]   quidem] enim **KF**   permisi] feci **y**   transmissa **W**[b]   **8** igitur] ergo **y**   videlicet *ex* vidi *corr.* **F**   et[2] *om.* **y**   michi[2] *om.* **y**   ac] et **y** **9** pertinet **y**   **10** ipsarum] animarum **KF**   **11** licite *om.* **y KF**   te[1] *post* possem *tpt.* **KF**   tuam *supra lin.* **q**   tuo *om.* **F**   **12** diminuitur **W**[b]   ad *om.* **W**[b] accrescant **F**   plus *ante* inflammaberis *add.* **W**[b]

diuino igne caritatis mee. **13** Veni igitur et noli tardare! Veni non cum superbia solita et mundana pompa sed cum omni humilitate et ardenti caritate! Et postquam sic veneris, extirpa, euelle et dissipa omnia vicia de curia tua! **14** Remoue eciam a te consilia carnalium et mundanorum amicorum tuorum et sequere humiliter consilia spiritualia amicorum meorum. Aggredere ergo et noli timere, consurge viriliter et induere fortitudine confidenter! **15** Incipe renouare Ecclesiam meam, quam ego acquisiui meo proprio sanguine, ut renouetur et spiritualiter reducatur ad pristinum statum suum sanctum, quia iam nunc magis veneratur lupanar quam sancta mea Ecclesia.

16 Si autem non obedieris predicte voluntati mee, firmiter scias, quod tali sentencia et spirituali iusticia comdempnaberis a me coram tota mea celesti curia, **17** quali condempnatur et punitur temporaliter prelatus degradandus, qui publice exuitur sacris vestibus pontificalibus glorie cum pudore et malediccione et repletur ignominia et confusione. **18** Sic ego faciam tibi, nam deponam te de celesti gloria, et omnia, que modo tibi sunt ad pacem et honorem, erunt tibi ad malediccionem et eternam confusionem, **19** et quilibet inferni dyabolus rapiet morsellum de anima tua, quamuis ipsa immortalis et inconsumptibilis sit, et pro benediccione repleberis eterna malediccione. Et quamdiu paciar te inobedientem michi, quamdiu prosperaberis.

20 Verumptamen, fili Gregori, adhuc moneo te, ut humiliter conuertaris ad me, et obedi consilio meo, patris tui et creatoris tui, quia si tu predicto modo obedieris michi, ego ut pater pius misericorditer suscipiam te. **21** Aggredere igitur viriliter viam iusticie et prosperaberis. Noli contempnere diligentem te, quia et si tu obedieris, faciam tecum misericordiam et benedicam te ac eciam vestiam te et ornabo te preciosis ornamentis pontificalibus veri pape et induam te me ipso ita, quod tu eris in me et ego ero in te et glorificaberis in eternum." **22** Hiis autem sic visis et auditis hec visio disparuit.

---

13 igitur] ergo y   extirpe **q F**   et *ante* euelle *add.* y   et[4] supra lin. **F 14** tuorum...meorum *om.* **q**   spiritualium **W** ᵇ   fortitudinem **KF**   et *ante* confidenter *add.* **W** ᵇ   **15** proprio meo y   ad] in **W** ᵇ   *ex* suum statum *corr.* **F**   iam *om.* **K** add. **F**²   ecclesia mea **W** ᵇ   **16** tu *ante* non *add.* **W** ᵇ   mea *om.* **W** ᵇ *post* curia *tpt.* **F   17** condempnabatur **F   18** ego *om.* y   tibi modo **KF   19** rapiat y **q** inobediente **W** ᵇ   **20** meo] mei **W** ᵇ **q**   tui[2] *om.* y   **21** Aggredere] Egredere **W** ᵇ igitur] ergo y   me *post* contempnere *add.* **W** ᵇ   et[2] *om.* **W** ᵇ   te[3] *om.* **W** ᵇ   et[4] *om.* **yq**   ero *om.* **W** ᵇ   gloriaberis **W** ᵇ   **22** Hiis] Hii **W** ᵇ

*Reuelacio quarta, quam domina Brigida misit domino pape in mense
Iulii anno Domini MCCCLXXIII. Et ipsa scripsit cuidam heremite, qui
olim fuit episcopus, qui tunc erat cum domino papa super hoc in
Auinione.*

1 Dominus noster Iesus Christus dixit michi, domine episcope, quod
ego scriberem vobis infrascripta verba, que debetis ostendere summo
pontifici:
   2 "Papa petit signum. Dic ei, quod Pharisei petierunt signum. Quibus respondi, quod sicut Ionas fuit in ventre ceti tribus diebus et tribus noctibus, sic ego, filius virginis, fui in terra mortuus tribus diebus
et tribus noctibus. Post vero signum promissum ego filius Dei fui
passus, mortuus et sepultus et resurrexi et ascendi in gloriam meam. 3
Sic papa iste Gregorius accepit signum ammonicionis mee, ut saluet
animas. Faciat ergo opere que honoris sunt mei et laboret, quomodo
saluentur anime et ut ecclesia mea veniat in pristinum statum et meliorem disposicionem, et tunc experietur signum et fructum eterne consolacionis. 4 Secundum habebit signum, quod nisi obedierit verbis
meis et venerit in Ytaliam, non solum perdet temporalia sed eciam spiritualia et senciet tribulacionem cordis, quamdiu viuet. Et quamuis
quandoque cor eius videatur habere releuamen, tamen remorsus consciencie et interna tribulacio remanebit sibi. 5 Tercium signum est,
quod ego Deus loquor cum una muliere verba mirabilia. Ad quid hoc et
ad quem fructum, nisi ad animarum utilitatem et ut mali emendentur
et ut boni fiant meliores?
   6 De discordia vero inter papam et Barnabonem respondeo, quod
ultra modum est michi odiosa, quia infinite anime de illa periclitantur.

Cap. X *cf IV: 143.* Alfonso, *Informaciones §§ 48, Conscripcio, p. 87.* 2 petit signum
cf. Jönsson, Alfonso, p. 53.

X: **W**ᵇ **yq KF**
R domina] beata **KF**   Brigida] birgitta **q** F B **y** K   scribit **W**ᵇ
super hoc *om.* **KF** super hiis **W**ᵇ   in auinione] auinioni *ut videtur* **K** *om.* **F**¹ auinione **F**²   **2** sic ego...noctibus *om.* **F**   fui] fuit **y**   et *ante* mortuus *add.* **W**ᵇ
et⁴ *om.* **q**   sic *ante* ascendi *add.* **W**ᵇ   **3** iste papa **y** ipse papa **KF**   opera **K**
      mei sunt **yq**   in] ad **y** F   **4** nisi] si non **KF**   temporalia perdet **K F**
videtur **y KF**   sue *post* consciencie *add.* **y**   salutem *ante* utilitatem *add.* **F**
      meliores fiant **y**   **6** De *om.* **q**

7 Ideo placitum est michi, quod concordia fiat, nam eciam si papa expulsus esset a papatu suo, melius esset, quod papa humiliaret se et faceret concordiam, quacumque occasione posset fieri, antequam tot anime perirent in eternam dampnacionem. **8** De emendacione vero regni Francie non habebit scire, antequam personaliter papa venerit in Ytaliam.

9 Itaque sicut si staret patibulum, super quod penderet funis, quem ex una parte infiniti traherent, ex alia vero non nisi unus, sic dampnacio animarum aperta est et quasi ad illam plerique laborant. **10** Ideo papa iste respiciat ad me unum, quia, licet omnes dissuadeant ei venire Romam et obsistant, in quantum possunt, confidat in me uno et iuuabo eum et nulli preualebunt in eum. **11** Sed sicut pulli in nido, veniente matre, eleuant se et clamant et gaudent, sic ego gaudenter occurram ei et eleuabo eum et ad animam et ad corpus honorabo."

12 Item ait Dominus: "Quoniam dubitat papa, an debeat venire Romam pro reformacione pacis et ecclesie mee, volo quod omnino veniat in proximo sequenti autumpno, et sciat eciam, quod nichil gracius potest michi facere, quam quod in Ytaliam veniat.'

(XI)

Paulo ante mortem habuit sponsa Christi subscriptam reuelacionem a Christo, que tangit dictum dominum papam Gregorium super aduentum ad Romam.

1 Contigit quinque diebus ante diem obitus domine Brigide, sepedicte sponse Christi, quod apparuit ei dominus noster Iesus Christus ante

Cap. XI *cf. VII: 31 (see pp. 28-29). Jönsson, 'On the so-called Tractatus', p. 21.*

7 eciam] et W^b   papa^1 ipsa y ipse KF   papa^2 ipse KF   fieri posset F
8 papa *om*. q   ueniret y   9 si sicut W^b   super] supra W^b   non *om*. W^b
10 omnes licet W^b   in *ante* R o m a m *add.* y   obstant KF   in quantum] quantumcumque y quantum KF   uno] unum q   ego *ante* iuuabo *add.* K F
11 ad^2 *om*. q KF   12 et^2 *om*. W^b

Rubrica cap. XI: W^b yq   § 1-13 W^b
R Christi *om*. W^b   aduentu W^b

altare, quod erat in camera sua, et leta facie se ostendens ei dixit: **2** "Ego feci tibi, sicut sponsus solet facere, qui abscondit se a sponsa sua, ut ab ea ardencius desideretur. Sic ego te non visitaui consolacionibus isto tempore, quia tempus probacionis tunc erat. **3** Ideo nunc iam probata procede et para te, quia iam tempus est, quod adimpleatur illud, quod promiseram tibi, scilicet quod ante altare meum in monacam vestieris et consecraberis. Et amodo reputaberis non solum sponsa mea, sed monaca et mater in Waztcnum. **4** Verumptamen scito, quod corpus tuum depones hic in Roma, donec venerit in locum sibi paratum."

5 Et conuersus ad Romam quasi conquerendo dixit: "O Roma mea, o Roma mea, papa contempnit me et non attendit ad verba mea, sed recipit dubia pro certis. Ideo non amplius audiet fistulam meam, quia tempus misericordie posuit in arbitrio suo."

6 Et post aliqua alia verba subiunxit dominus et dixit sponse: **7** "Scias, quod venient homines illi, quando michi placuerit, qui cum suauitate et gaudio recipient verba ista celestium reuelacionum, que hactenus tibi facte sunt, et complebuntur omnia illa, que dicta sunt. **8** Et licet multis subtracta est gracia propter ingratitudinem eorum, alii tamen venient, qui surgent in loco illorum et obtinebunt graciam meam."

10 Hiis autem dictis et multis aliis, que hic non scribuntur, mencionem fecit et ordinacionem dicta sponsa Christi aliquarum personarum secum existencium, quas ante mortem coram Deo se vidisse dicebat.

11 Post ista audita subiunxit Dominus dicens: "In mane diei quinti postquam sumpseris sacramenta, conuoca sigillatim personas tecum existentes, quas tibi nominaui modo, et dicas illa, que facere debent. **12** Et sic inter verba et manus eorum venies ad monasterium tuum, id est in gaudium meum, et corpus tuum locabitur in Waztenum." **13** Deinde appropinquante die quinta in ipsa aurora iterum apparuit ei Christus consolando eam. Dicta vero missa et sacramentis perceptis cum maxima deuocione et reuerencia inter verba et manus predictarum personarum emisit spiritum.

Visio ostensa sponse pertimenda de quodam summo pontifice circa mortem eiusdem pontificis.

1 Paulo ante mortem cuiusdam pontificis mirabili casu comburebantur campane Sancti Petri in Roma. Que audiens sponsa stupefacta orabat. Et tunc apparuit ei Christus dicens: **2** "Vere, filia, magnum signum est istud, nam scriptum est, quod elementa omnia quasi compaciebantur michi in morte, quando splendorem et solitum effectum suum retraxerunt. **3** Sic elementa et creature quandoque pugnant et iudicant pro Deo et ostendunt in cursibus <suis> iram <Dei> et signa euentuum futurorum, sed nunc ecce comburuntur campane et quasi clamant omnes: **4** 'Dominus mortuus est. Dominus pontifex recessit. Sit dies ista benedicta, sed non dominus iste benedictus!' O mirabile! Ubi enim omnes clamare deberent: 'Viuat diu et viuat feliciter iste dominus!', ibi clamant et gaudenter dicunt: **5** 'Descendat et non consurgat!'. Nec mirum, nam ipse, qui clamare debuerat: 'Venite, et inuenietis requiem animarum vestrarum!', ipse clamat: **6** 'Venite et inuenietis me in pompa et ambicione plus quam Salomonem! Venite ad curiam meam et exhaurite bursas vestras, et inuenietis perdicionem animarum vestrarum!" Sic enim clamat exemplo et facto. Et ideo iam appropinquat tempus ire, et iudicabo eum sicut dissipatorem gregis Petri. O, o, quale iudicium instat ei! Verumptamen, si adhuc voluerit conuerti ad me, ego occurram ei in media via sicut pius pater."

Clement VI

Cap. XII *cf VI: 96.*   summo pontifice *sc. Urban V (cf. Alfonso, Informaciones §* *11)*

XII: **W**[b]
R *cf. rubr. cap. XIII in app. crit.* **3** suis *et* Dei *addidi Rev. VI: 96 secutus.*

Visio, quam habuit sponsa Christi de iudicio anime cuiusdam summi pontificis defuncti.

1 Videbat sponsa quasi unam personam pontificis vestitam scapulari, que stabat in domo luto platearum respersa, cuius domus tectum fere iacebat super cerebrum dicte persone compressum, **2** et Ethiopes nigri habentes uncos et alia instrumenta nocendi circumuallabant domum, sed non valebant tangere personam illam, licet terrebant eam terrore maximo. **3** Et tunc audiui vocem dicentem michi: "Hec est anima illius magni pontificis, quem tu nosti. Domus enim ista est retribucio eius spiritualis, nam aliqua mundana tractabat et ideo remuneracio eius nondum lucida est, donec in purgatorio mundetur et dealbetur spiritualibus oracionibus et caritate Dei. **4** Quod vero tectum quasi comprimit cerebrum eius, signum misterii est, quia tectum significat caritatem Dei, que quanto maior est, tanto lacior est et sublimior ad spiritualia et feruorem Dei, **5** sed quia caritas anime huius in aliquibus mundialibus operibus ardebat et magis sequebatur voluntatem propriam, ideo tectum, quod luminosum et altum est electis Dei, angustum est sibi, donec sanguine filii Dei et celestis curie interuentu dilatetur. **6** Quod vero anima induta est scapulari, signum est, quod studuit se conformare religioni sue monastice et vocacioni sue, sed non tantum conatus est, quod esset exemplar proficiencium et forma perfectorum.

7 Nunc autem licitum est tibi scire tria de operibus, que fecit in vita sua, propter que nunc patitur penam. Primum est, quod fecit quandam inobedienciam contra Deum et conscienciam suam, de quo contricionem habuit et remorsum consciencie sue. **8** Secundum est,

---

Cap. XIII *cf. IV:144* **R** summi pontificis *sc. Urban V.*

XIII: **W**[b] **yq KF**
R Visio...defuncti] Visio ostensa christi pertimenda de quodam summo pontifice circa mortem eiusdem pontificis **y** (*cf. rubr. cap. XII*)   ostensa *post* visio *del.* **q**   habuit sponsa christi] sponsa habuit **W**[b]   de quo eciam habetur sexto libro ca. xcvi *post* defuncti *add* **F**   **1** sponsa *om.* **W**[b]   astabat **yq**   **2** uncinos **W**[b]   et[2] ac   **3** audiuit **W**[b]   illius] illa **W**[b]   in *om.* **y**   **4** quasi] ita **y** *om.* **K F**   que] et **y**   est[3] *post* sublimior *tpt.* **W**[b]   ad *ante* feruorem *add.* **F**   **5** in *om.* **W**[b]   **6** scapulari **y**   **7** est licitum **KF**   quo] qua *ut videtur* **W**[b]

quod dispensabat in aliquibus cum quibusdam propter carnalem amorem sequendo voluntatem suam. Tercium est, quod dissimulabat aliqua, ne offenderet quos diligebat, que corrigere potuisset.

9 Verumptamen scias, quod anima ista non est cum illis, qui descendunt in infernum nec cum illis, qui veniunt ad grauiora examina purgatorii sed cum illis qui cotidie festinanter appropinquant gracie et visioni maiestatis Dei omnipotentis."

8 cum quibusdam *om.* **q**   quibusdam] quibus **W** **b**   **9** est *post* illis[3] *add.* **yq** **K** festinanter appropinquant] festinant **q**   omnipotentis *om.* **W** **b**

4. Results and discussion

4.1. The title and the content of the *Tractatus*

In modern works of scholarship, the *Tractatus* has been referred to as either the *Tractatus de summis pontificibus*, as did Prior Peter once in his testimony to the canonization commission (p. 14), or as the *Liber ad summos pontifices*, which was the title originally used by the Confessor General of Vadstena Monastery, Magnus Petri, in a letter dated 1384-91.[58] Neither of these titles has manuscript authority, however. As established above, the authentic title is much longer and indicates clearly the scope and aim of the collection:

> Reuelaciones infrascriptas habuit in visione spirituali diuinitus deuota ancilla Christi sancte memorie Domina Brigida, principissa de regno Suecie, stando in oracione. Que diriguntur ad summos pontifices Clementem VI, Innocencium VI, Urbanum V, Gregorium XI. Que tractant de reducendo Sedem Apostolicam et Romanam curiam ad Romam et de reformacione ecclesie ex precepto Dei omnipotentis.

In the *Tractatus*, there are thus revelations to popes Clement VI, Inno-cent VI, Urban V and Gregory XI concerning the return of the Papal See to Rome and a reform of the Church. Alfonso seems to have been most anxious to maintain the authority of the collection: St. Bridget speaks as directed by God the Almighty, *ex precepto Dei omnipotentis*; as Alfonso had proved in his previous work, the *Epistola solitarii*, she is a pious servant of Christ, *deuota ancilla Christi*, but also a princess from the Kingdom of Sweden, *principissa de regno Suecie* (cf. his *In-formaciones* § 3 and his *Prologus Libri Celestis* § 2),[59] so that nobody would confuse humility with obscurity.

To be sure, it might have seemed natural to assume that when Prior Peter spoke about the "tractatus de summis pontificibus" in his testimony, it was the title of the collection he gave, but since we find another title in the manuscripts, we must conclude that this was not the case. Perhaps Peter felt that the original title was too long to be used, or it was not really a title, and just referred to the work as "the thematic collection concerning popes", which seems to be the most adequate translation of Peter's words.

In the printed editions, the *Tractatus* was integrated into the *corpus reuelacionum*, which meant that the duplicate revelations were not entered. Revelation II became IV: 136, etc., as showed in the table on p. 19. The title of the original *Tractatus* was enlarged by the addi-

---

[58]Edited by Undhagen, 'Une source', § XVII. For the date, see p. 218.
[59]Jönsson, *Alfonso of Jaén*, pp. 185 and 168.

tion of the original chapter heading for rev. II and used as a rubric to IV: 136. *Domina Brigida* was changed into *Sancta Birgitta.*

As far as the question of the content of the *Tractatus* is concerned, it has been demonstated above that the Florence and London manuscripts, which have been supposed to show that Alfonso's original compilation contained twenty-one or fifty-seven revelations respectively, did not do so, but in actual fact can be used as evidence for the same thirteen-revelations-version that we find in the source manuscripts of the *corpus reuelacionum.*

In this third collection, Alfonso resorted to re-editing *four* revelations from the *Liber Celestis* in addition to *nine* unpublished ones. Alfonso had proceeded in a similar way when editing the *Liber Celestis Imperatoris ad Reges,* which in his redaction consisted of twenty-four re-edited revelations and thirty-four thitherto un-edited ones.

The revelations of the *Tractatus* are in the main arranged chronologically: Alfonso begins with the revelation to Pope Clement VI that Bridget had received in 1348. This revelation had already been published in the *Liber Celestis* as VI: 63, but Alfonso now revises the heading, adding information about the dating and about who was entrusted with the task of bringing the message to Pope Clement. In the end of the revelation, there is an allusion to the grandiose beginning of the prologue to Book I (*stupor et mirabilia facta sunt in terra nostra*) written by St. Bridget's earlier confessor, the learned theologian Master Mathias, who vouches there for her divine calling and the authenticity of the revelations.

Rev. II concerns Clement's successor, Innocent VI. We are not given any information in Alfonso's other works, the *Informaciones* and the *Conscripcio,* about contacts with this pope, and the entry here gives the impression of being a space-filler. However, judging from the last lines, Bridget seems to have sent books of revelations to him.

Revs. III-V concern Pope Urban V. Rev. III had already been published as IV: 49. This revelation, too, is now given a new heading with information about where ("in Sancta Maria Maiori in Roma") and when ("Una die antequam papa Urbanus intraret Romam", sc. 15 October 1367) Bridget had it. In the *Liber Celestis,* the message itself was all-important; in the *Tractatus* it is felt to be important to give details about the historical context. Rev. V is the one St. Bridget in person handed over to the pope in Montefiascone, when he was on his way back to Avignon. The Virgin Mary is very displeased with the pope, and tells him that he will be punished if he fails her and returns to Avignon.

Revs. VI-XI are addressed to Pope Gregory XI or are about him. The message is the same as before: removal of the Papal See from Avignon back to Rome and reform of the Church. The pope was, however, good at procrastination, as is witnessed by the revelations, and gradually, a tone of aggressive frustration becomes clearly noticeable. In the headings, we are given some information about the context in which the revelations were received and this is supplemented by Alfonso's more detailed report in the *Informaciones* and the *Conscripcio*. We are, thus, in a good position to observe the developments all the way until St. Bridget's death. The last revelation to Gregory, rev. XI, is the one she received five days before her death and which had been published in the *Liber celestis* as VII: 31 (see above pp. 28-29). Christ appears and complains about the pope who does not listen to his words and leaves Rome in the lurch, but now he will get no more messages.

Rev. XII-XIII do not fit in chronologically—they are about the judgement of Clement VI and Urban V—but have been placed in conclusion as a warning to neglectful and disobedient popes, a message clearly brought out by the headings of these revelations.

4.2. The aim and the date of the *Tractatus*

It has been assumed that after the editing of the *Liber celestis*, which is a voluminous and heterogeneous collection, Alfonso began to make compilations in which the revelations were arranged according to subject matter, in order to make St. Bridget's revelations well-known and appreciated in wider circles.[60] The *Liber celestis imperatoris ad reges* may well have been compiled for this reason, but the editing of the *Tractaus* was certainly motivated by much more specific and urgent reasons, as is clearly indicated by the title: this collection was an element in Alfonso's efforts to gain support for Pope Urban VI in his conflict with the anti-pope Clement VII, who had been elected after the cardinals had declared Urban's election null and void. The *Tractatus* is closely linked to the *Informaciones*, the memorandum Alfonso wrote (probably for an inquest in November 1379) to defend the validity of Urban VI's election as pope.[61] In the *Informaciones*, Alfonso refers to eight of the thirteen *Tractatus* revelations in support of his argumentation. One line of argument in the *Informaciones* is that God had revealed in his revelations to St. Bridget that it is His will that the pope reside in Rome. Her insistence on Rome as home of the popes, the vilification of everything connected with Avignon, the call for reform, the violent protest against simony and a clear anti-cardinalism were messages with renewed relevancy after the out-break of the great schism,

---

[60]Schück, p. 20-21, Undhagen, *Rev.I*, p. 22. Nyberg in *Birgitta of Sweden*, pp. 38-39.
[61]Jönsson, *Alfonso of Jaén*, pp. 72-74.

and was particularly applicable after Clement's departure for Avignon in the summer of 1379, when the anti-Avignon revelations gained relevance in a new context.

The *terminus ante quem* for the dating of the *Tractatus* is, of course, January 30th, 1380, the date of Prior Peter's deposition. In a previous work, I suggested that the fact that Alfonso in the *Informaciones* did not refer to the revelations in the *Tractatus* by title and number indicated that they had not been published yet.[62] As the edition above shows, that argument is totally irrelevant, since the revelations are not numbered in the *Tractatus*, and it is thus perfectly possible that the *Tractatus* was compiled before the *Informaciones* was written, i. e., somewhat earlier in the autumn of 1379.

4.3. The codification of the revelations

As mentioned above, the *Tractatus* is not included in Alfonso's redactions of the St. Bridget's revelations, and the reason for this has been discussed, for instance, by Schück and Undhagen, who suggest that it was omitted "by way of ecclesiastical precaution" (above pp. 15-16).[63] This is a suggestion that gives rise to questions rather than answers: why on earth did Alfonso compile a work he is supposed to have considered suspicious? Why did he consider these revelations unobjectionable when he referred to them in his *Informaciones*, but inopportune when he made the codification? Why did Prior Peter himself refer to this very collection in his statement to the canonization commission, if there were the faintest risk that it could be considered suspicious? These are difficult questions to answer.

Before we try and find the motives for the exclusion, the question of the dating of the codification has to be scrutinized. To be sure, Undhagen dates Alfonso's second redaction to "about 1380". If we take this as meaning "1379 or later", it is reasonable to speculate about why the *Tractatus* is missing in the codified books of revelations. Undhagen's point of departure for the dating is based on the assumption that it was the *first* Alfonso redaction that was submitted to the second papal commission in 1378/79. Undhagen's reason for assuming this is that since "the first examining commission does not seem to have had any objections to the revelations they had been given to examine, it would seem unlikely that Alfonso would have found it necessary to revise the text of the 1377 redaction."[64] Since, however, the *second* redaction can have been finished as early as 1377, we cannot

---

[62]Jönsson, *Alfonso of Jaén*, p. 76.
[63]Undhagen, *Rev. I*, p. 25.
[64]Undhagen, *Rev. I*, p. 14.

exclude the possibility that it was this redaction that was presented to the papal authorities. Be that as it may. Even if it was the first redaction that was presented, it is quite clear that the second edition must have been finished not later than 16 September 1379, when Alfonso in his testimony for the canonization commission referred to the *Epistola solitarii*,[65] in which there are references not only to the *Liber celestis* but also to the *Liber celestis imperatoris ad reges* and the *Sermo angelicus*. Thus, it is perfectly possible that Alfonso's work of codification was finished *before* the *Tractatus* was compiled and this is why it was not included. Generally speaking, there is no reason whatsoever to assume that the father confessors found parts of Bridget's revelations objectionable and thus had to be suppressed.

4.4. Alfonso's rôle as editor

Much has been written about how St. Bridget's message was transmitted—and perhaps transformed—by her father confessors when translating and editing her revelations.[66] There has been a tendency in recent scholarship to attach great importance to Alfonso's rôle as editor of the revelations. No wonder, since Christ—or Bridget— entrusted him with this task in terms that seemingly gave him quite extensive authority to make a revision (*Rev. ex.* 49):

> trade omnes libros reuelacionum eorundem verborum meorum episcopo meo heremite, qui conscribat et obscura elucidet et catholicum sensum spiritus mei teneat.

All books of revelation were thus to be handed over to Alfonso, who would elucidate them and guard the Catholic sense of Christ's spirit. How did Alfonso fulfil that task? Diverse answers have been advanced. In his edition of book V, which, to be sure, was revealed to Bridget many years earlier when she was still in Sweden, Bergh concluded that Alfonso may not even have read much of that book.[67] On the other hand, Gilkær in his study of St. Bridget's and Alfonso's political ideas and attitudes used Alfonso's compilation, the *Liber celestis imperatoris ad reges,* as a source to *Alfonso's*, not *Bridget's*, ideas.[68] In so doing, he was inspired *inter alia* by Aili's research. By comparing some revelations that are available in two different editions, viz. in the *Liber celestis* and in the *Liber celestis imperatoris ad reges,* Aili claims to have pin-pointed some examples of Alfonsine manipulation with

---

[65]*A & P*, p. 375.
[66]A recent contribution is Ellis, 'The Divine Message and its Human Agents'.
[67]Bergh, *Rev. V*, pp 17-18.
[68]P. 22

the Bridgettine message, for instance the following: when Alfonso re-publishes Rev. IV: 4 in the *Liber celestis imperatoris ad reges* (ch. 13), he adds in the rubric and in the revelation itself the information that the person in question was "a queen", whereas, writes Aili, "the older version of the Revelations text offers no such information at all".[69] Here Aili seems, however, to have jumped to conclusions. To be sure, it is true that it is not *explicitly* stated in the original version that the lady mentioned is a queen, but other details given clearly indicate that that was the case: for instance in § 29, we learn that the lady wears a crown and is dressed in purple.[70] Another fact pointing in the same direction is that a princess, St. Elizabeth of Hungary, is mentioned as model for the lady, since that saint got greater consolation and a *more sublime crown*, when living in poverty than if she had remained in worldly honour and consolation.

In this context it is interesting to see what liberties—if any—Alfonso took when quoting from St. Bridget. In the *Conscripcio* there is a long quotation from the *Tractatus*:

Tractatus, rev. 7:

> **16** ..."Item dic episcopo meo heremite, quod claudat istam litteram et si-gillet eam et postea scribat in alia papiro copiam eius et ostendat eandem copiam apertam illi abbati, nuncio pape et Nolano comiti, ut ipsi legant illam et sciant, quid continetur in ea. **17** Postquam vero ipsi eam lege-rint, dimittat eis supradictam litteram clausam, sigillatam, quam ipsi sta-tim mittant pape Gregorio sine mora. Sed copiam illam apertam post-quam legerint, non dimittat eis, sed volo, quod dilaceret et rumpat eam coram oculis eorum in frusta. **18** Quia sicut littera illa, que est una, dila-cerabitur in multa frusticula, sic nisi papa tempore et anno prefixo ve-nerit in Ytaliam, terre Ecclesie, que sub una eius obediencia et subiec-cione modo eidem obediunt, diuidentur in plures partes in manus tyran-norum.

Quoted in *Conscripcio*, p. 87:

> [16] Dic Alfonso heremite olim episcopo, quod scribat hanc revelacio-nem et clausam et sigillatam portet ad illum abbatem, quam ipse statim mittat ad papam. Scribat eciam ipse Alfonsus dicte revelacionis copiam in papiro et portet secum apertam et ostendat eam dicto abbati, ut ipse abbas eam legat, et videat quid continetur in ea. [17] Postea vero in pre-sencia dicti abbatis ipse Alfonsus dilaceret ipsam copiam in frusticula, [18] quia, sicut ipsa revelacio tunc dilacerabatur in frusticula, ita, si pa-pa non veniat tempore sibi assignato ad Romam, omnes terre Ecclesie, que modo sub una obediencia sunt, dilacerabuntur in frusticula per ma-nus tyrannorum et inimicorum Ecclesie.

---

[69]'St. Birgitta and the Text of the Revelationes', pp. 86-87.
[70]Personal communication from Prof. Bergh.

A few remarks can be made: in the quotation, the name of the bishop and hermit is given, just as in the example above from the *Liber celestis imperatoris ad reges*, the identity of the lady was clarified by the information that she was a queen. § 17 is shortened, the instructions about sending the letter to the pope are omitted in the quotation, but Alfonso tells us a little later in the text that the Count of Nola brought the letter to the pope, so that information is not really missing. There are also signs of slight stylistic revision, as in the *quod*-sentence in § 16, which in Alfonso's *Conscripcio* version is much more elegant than in the original version. What we can learn from this comparison is that to be sure Alfonso did not quote word for word, but that he nevertheless was quite close to the actual wording and did not change the message itself.

Generally speaking, I am very sceptical about attempts to make Alfonso a moulder, not only a transmitter, of Bridget's message. However, in the absence of an edition of the *Liber celestis imperatoris ad reges*,[71] it would be premature to try and make a general assessment of Alfonso's rôle as editor, so I feel justified in confining myself to repeting some remarks I have made earlier on the basis of an examination of the *Tractatus*.

In the *Tractatus*, Alfonso's influence can be recognized primarily in the selection and presentation of the texts. Alfonso wrote new chapter headings for revelations I and XI that changed the emphasis considerably, above pp. 22 and 28-29, and omitted two passages in ch. 11 that were irrelevant in the new context.[72] Obviously, he felt he had the freedom, or possibly the duty—in the above-mentioned *rev. ex.* 49, he had been given the office of an evangelist[73]—to apply St. Bridget's principles in the way he felt most suitable and adapt them to new contexts. As regards the great schism, there could not be any doubt about what position Bridget would have taken, had she lived. The return of the popes from Avignon to Rome and a reform of the Church were causes that had motivated her all her life. *

[71] Dr. Aili is working on an edition of that book.
[72] 'On the so-called *Tractatus*', p. 27
[73] *Filius Dei loquebatur ad sponsam dicens: "--- Item dic eidem heremite [sc. Alfonso], quod faciat et impleat officium euangeliste."*
* I am most grateful to Dr. Carole Gillis, who has revised my English.

STUDIA GRAECA ET LATINA LUNDENSIA
Ediderunt Birger Bergh et Jerker Blomqvist

1. Arne Jönsson, *Alfonso of Jaén. His Life and Works with Critical Editions of the* Epistola Solitarii, *the* Informaciones *and the* Epistola Serui Christi. 1989. 207 pp.

2. Bengt-Arne Roos, *Synesius of Cyrene. A Study in His Personality.* 1991. 157 pp.

3. Brita Larsson, *Johannes Magnus' Latin Letters. A Critical Edition with Introduction and Commentary.* 1992. v + 193 pp.

4. Lars Nyberg, *Unity and Coherence. Studies in Apollonius Rhodius'* Argonautica *and the Alexandrian Epic Tradition.* 1992. xviii + 182 pp.

5. Dimitrios Karadimas, *Sextus Empiricus against Aelius Aristides. The Conflict between Philsophy and Rhetoric in the Second Century A. D.* 1996. xx + 270 pp.

6. Arne Jönsson, *St. Bridget's Revelations to the Popes. An edition of the so-called* Tractatus de summis pontificibus. 1996. 69 pp.

—